Coming Home
to Raise Your Children

Coming Home
to Raise Your Children

A Survival Guide for Moms

Christine M. Field

Fleming H. Revell
A Division of Baker Book House Co
Grand Rapids, Michigan 49516

© 1995 by Christine M. Field

Published by Fleming H. Revell
a division of Baker Book House Company
P.O. Box 6287, Grand Rapids, MI 49516-6287

Second printing, October 1996

Printed in the United States of America

Library of Congress Cataloging-in-Publication Data

Field, Christine Moriarty, 1956–
    Coming home to raise your children : a survival guide for
moms / Christine Moriarty Field.
        p. cm.
    Includes bibliographical references.
    ISBN 0-8007-5567-7 (pbk.)
    1. Motherhood—United States. 2. Work and family—
United States. 3. Parenting—United States. I. Title.
    HQ759.F44 1995
    306.874'3—dc20   95-17435

Contents

Preface   7

1. Why I Went from Full-Time Lawyer to
   Full-Time Mom   9
2. Why Stay Home?   17
3. Can You Afford to Stay Home?   41
4. Making the Psychological
   Transformation   55
5. What Happened to My Self-Esteem?   73
6. You'll Always Be a Mother, but Your Kids
   Only Have One Childhood   81
7. The Mommy Wars   89
8. Getting Support from Your Husband   99
9. Finding Other Support   109
10. Getting It All Done   123
11. Finances   147
12. Taking Care of Ourselves   169
13. Enjoying the Family   183
14. On Home Schooling   195
15. In Praise of Sequencing   205

Notes   211

Preface

This is a book about being a mom. It was written by a mom, for moms, and for those who love them. We will talk about husbands, children, and friends, but this book is for moms.

There have been many moms who have profoundly influenced me, including my own. My mother-in-law, Rose Marie Field, has been a tremendous example of Christian womanhood. I am grateful to her and my father-in-law, Irving Field, for "adopting" me as their own daughter when I married their son.

Whether she knew it or not, my sister-in-law, Allenda Moriarty, became a surrogate mother to me after the early death of my own mother. I learned lessons about nurturing from her that I would not have learned otherwise. Her terrific daughters, Erin and Meghan, are evidence of her fine mothering.

I surveyed many women for this book about their decision to come home to raise their children. I asked them about their motivation and for their tips for survival. Their responses were a joy to read. They lifted my spirits and lightened my heart.

While these women come from varied backgrounds, they were all committed to mothering and were enthusiastic about the opportunity to be home to raise their children.

Their words inspired me, and their shared experience and wisdom is the heart of this book. These are the women of the Wheaton Evangelical Free Church, the Wheaton chapter of Mothers of Preschoolers (M.O.P.S.), St. Michael's Moms Plus Club, and the Du Page chapter of the Formerly Employed Mothers at the Leading Edge (F.E.M.A.L.E.). You women have been my lifeline in my journey of mothering, and I love you!

Finally, this book is lovingly dedicated to my husband, Mark, and our children, Clare, Caitlin, and Grace. You are the family I thought I would never have—an unanticipated turn in my life's journey that has brought me such joy and happiness.

1

Why I Went from Full-Time Lawyer to Full-Time Mom

A few years ago, I spent my days dealing with murderers, drug dealers, and burglars—and I loved it. It was interesting for me to hear their thoughts and sometimes bizarre rationalizations for their behavior. One young mother shook her baby to death because the baby cried all night, and the mother had to get up for work in the morning. Scores of drug dealers talked about how their difficult backgrounds had brought them to crime. But a common thread ran through all the stories of the felons I dealt with every day—the lack of an effective family structure when they were growing up.

After the birth of our second child, I began to feel the real incongruence of my roles. An afternoon visit to the jail to see clients was followed by a trip to our day care provider to pick up our two beautiful little girls. At that time I loved both of my worlds. Now my heart leans only toward home.

We have been truly blessed. After several years of dealing with infertility and miscarriage, we adopted a beautiful infant girl through a private agency. On very short notice we became an instant family. Acting as if my life could go on without skipping a beat, I moved a portable crib into my office and had a wonderful secretary who would cuddle our daughter while I went to court. Back at the office, I held her, pacing and swaying while I talked to clients. I sometimes had to ask a client to hold her for a minute while I did something else.

When our first daughter was two months old, I accepted a new job, one that did not involve the sixty-hour work week of private legal practice. My hours were generally cut back, except when I was trying a jury trial. Fortunately, I had found a wonderful Christian day care provider, Jodie Forbes, who genuinely loved our daughter. God was clearly looking out for us when he brought Jodie to our family. In fact, she taught me much of what I know about mothering, as I was ill-prepared for the job, and she has remained a life-long friend. What I learned from her helped me do a good job with our children when I came home full-time to raise them. She did what it says in Titus 2:4–5—the older women "can train the younger women to love their husbands and children, to be self-controlled and pure, to be busy at home, to be kind"—and I will be forever grateful to her.

Even with Jodie's help, however, I felt that neither of my jobs was being adequately served. When I was working, I wanted to be home. When I was home, I worried about the people whose lives and liberty had been entrusted to my care. Something had to change.

Sometimes God has to get my attention through a whack on the side of the head. That whack came in the form of our biological daughter, who was born seventeen months after our first daughter. We had two babies drinking from bottles and in diapers. The oldest was barely walking, and the new baby had colic. We knew we had been blessed, but during the early months, we sometimes felt we were *too* blessed.

Some women splendidly adjust to the rigors of being a working mother. I did not. I tried to have it all, but I was kidding myself, and my family was suffering. I heartily applaud the women who are successful at this, but I was not among their ranks.

As if God wasn't sure I had heard his message to go home, he sent me another whack on the head—a major, super job change for my husband. The offer was one he could not pass up and involved moving to a great community some eighty miles away from my practice. After a few months of arguing, praying, negotiating, and praying some more, we moved.

It took me a few months to wind up my cases, and I commuted a few days a week while doing so, but soon everything was completed, and I found myself plopped down in my new life. I had no idea what to expect, and I had no clue what I was doing. I didn't know anyone in our neighborhood. No one knew me or my former profession. No one called me counselor. I became just another woman on the block with a couple of kids.

In those first few months at home, I was close to panic most of the time. I would look around our tiny, messy house at our tiny, messy children and think, "What happened to my life?" When my panic receded a bit, that thought was replaced by, "How am I going to manage this?"

I never thought I would be a full-time mom. I always assumed that when, and if, I had children, I would take a maternity leave and be chomping at the bit to return to work. One of my sisters had a pre-baby dream that I had a baby and put her in a shoe box in my closet and went back to work. I had also always assumed that the emotional division of my life would be that simple. But these preconceived expectations can change overnight.

With one child it was easy. Two parents getting three people out of the house in the morning was simple arithmetic. However, two parents getting four people going in the morning is more than doubly complicated.

First, there was the fatigue factor. Because I cut my hours back drastically after the adoption, I always had the energy to have fun with our first daughter. But children need quantity time, not just quality time, and the more children you have, the more time it takes.

When the second child came along, it was so exhausting to just meet their physical needs after meeting the demands of clients all day that our time together as a family suffered. After working all day, dropping off and picking up children, preparing dinner, giving baths, and doing some housework, all I wanted to do was crash on the couch. There was too little time for quantity time and too little energy for quality time.

Because of my reduced schedule after the adoption, I didn't miss any of our first daughter's milestones. But I did miss the fun (and the aggravation!) of full-time, day-to-day life with a child. I missed eating meals together, reading multiple stories on demand, kissing her hurts, and affirming her self-esteem on a daily basis.

When I quit my job, many colleagues and friends said, "You'll go crazy staying home!" Some asked, "How could you waste all that education?" But I haven't gone crazy, and our daughters are giving me a whole different kind of education. I am learning to pay attention to the beautiful, small details of life. I am learning patience. I am learning to relax and enjoy the too-short passage of childhood through the eyes of two small people who have some wonderful insights.

As for practicing law, there will always be acrimony and avarice. People will always have legal problems. It will all still be there when I have finished raising our babies. I will ask God for the wisdom, guidance, and discernment to know the right time to return. In my past profession, my days were full of seemingly weighty issues and hard decisions. Now, my days are full of small joys and wonders. I know in my heart that God has given us a wonderful gift and that full-time mothering is the highest and best use of my time and talents right now.

However, the realistic side of full-time mothering is that it's not always a bed of roses. I remember the first time I told my husband, "I don't want to be a mom today." One of our daughters had refused to go to sleep, and everyone was exhausted. "I don't mean I don't *ever* want to be a mom." I struggled to explain. "I just mean that for now. Like, right now. Like for the next couple of hours, even." The way he looked at me, I was certain he was about to call the child welfare authorities.

---

*W*hat do you enjoy most about being home?

The moments of intimacy with my kids.
—Susan Fenton

That moment passed, as they always do, and the next morning when I went to get our babies out of bed, I was once again in love with motherhood. I did feel guilty for having that feeling, but I've learned that guilt comes with the territory. I try to remember that my feelings about motherhood may change hourly, and that's okay. It's my commitment that must remain solid and stable.

We are definitely not the Cleaver family. We want only to be the Field family—a collection of interesting individuals with a strong bond. We want to be ourselves and to fashion our own unique way to be a family. For us that means taking meals together, attending church as a family, and taking time to enjoy our lives together. It has taken lots of time and hard work and some sacrifice to grow to the unity we now enjoy, but I believe this work is more important than anything I ever did in the marketplace. Fortunately, my husband agrees and totally supports me.

I find my full-time mothering to be all-consuming. I have learned that I cannot juggle many different activities. If my mind and schedule are too crowded, the whole family suffers. So I have determined what is most important for our family, and those are the things I concentrate on. Author Debbie Barr refers to prioritizing and simplifying your lifestyle as narrowing the channel to strengthen the stream. She says, "All major pursuits that are truly worth doing well in their proper season require a narrowing of the channel in order to strengthen the stream. If we chase too many big dreams at once or stretch our time and energy and resources across too many commitments, we do nothing well. We reap frustration instead of joy."[1]

> *What do you enjoy least about being home?*
>
> *The repetition of daily chores and the sameness of the scenery (especially during the winter).*
>
> —*Susan Fenton*

Have you heard the expression, "If Mama ain't happy, ain't nobody happy"? I believe that mothers are the barometer of emotional stability in the home. If Mom is distracted and being torn in a hundred different directions, her children and her husband will suffer. I see so many women who are so busy and so fragmented that they seem to just drag their way through their days going from one task to another. Granted we all have days and weeks where we are just hanging on by our fingernails, but where is the *joy* in that? We need to make sure that is not our normal condition. I don't want any regrets, no matter how our children turn out. I want to know in my heart that I have done the best job I can for them.

On bad days when I can't see beyond the pile of dirty diapers, the mediation of fifty fights before 9 A.M., or the peanut butter smeared on the wall, I have to remind myself that although some of these days are very long, the months of childhood are fleeing rather quickly. In *Home by Choice,* Dr. Brenda Hunter advises, "Become wholehearted about your life or you will miss the best that this period of your life has to offer."[2]

This book you are reading is an attempt to help you— the new mother, the not-yet mother, or the experienced mother—be wholehearted about all aspects of your life, build up a rich legacy of memories, and really have fun with this season of your life.

2

Why Stay Home?

If you ever want to hear words filled with passion and conviction, ask a dedicated mother at home why she chose her role. Mom Jewel Wolfe says, "My main dream was always to be a stay-at-home wife and mother. I wanted the joy and responsibility of raising our children, and I wanted to be home for them as much as possible. I did not want to entrust them to someone else's values or ideals for a great length of time." I surveyed a number of women on this issue and was heartened, warmed, and encouraged as these women spoke from their hearts about their commitment. You will read about the benefits of staying home throughout this chapter.

Benefits to the Children

Most of the benefits of your staying home will go to your child. For a young child, the opportunity to develop strong bonds with his or her mother is vitally important.

Solid Attachment to Mom

For the last few decades, researchers have been studying attachment theory, trying to determine what experiences or types of support children need in infancy to feel secure and loved.

Prior to the 1950s, most psychoanalysts followed Sigmund Freud's notion that drives, which originate in our unconscious minds, dictate all of our behavior. So psychoanalysts focused their study of behavior on the unconscious mind, which is not directly observable or measurable.

However in the early 1950s, a British researcher named John Bowlby began to study maternal deprivation—how separation from mothers affects children. In a report to the World Health Organization, Bowlby warned against separating children from their mothers, even less-than-perfect mothers. His reasons were that such deprivation put the children at increased risk for physical and mental illness. He thought that such separations thwarted the child's instinctual need (demonstrated by such behaviors as sucking, clinging, following mom) to keep mom close by.

And so *attachment theory* was born. In a landmark work on the subject, Bowlby outlined his underlying belief that a child needs a reliable, ongoing attachment to a primary caregiver and that he suffers, perhaps irreparably, if that attachment is interrupted or lost. Bowlby believed that "the young child's hunger for his mother's love and presence is as great as his hunger for food" and that her absence "inevitably generates a powerful sense of loss and anger."[1]

Bowlby was the first in a long line of experts whose research substantiates what mother wisdom has told us all along: Your baby needs you. In fact, her emotional attachment to you is crucial to her emotional development.

Another researcher and colleague of Bowlby's, Mary Ainsworth, picked up on this theory and expanded it. Her great contribution was to come up with a method of assessing or measuring relatedness. In her Baltimore lab in the 1960s, she devised a technique called the Strange Situation. One-year-old infants were taken to a lab with their mothers and observed as the mother separated from the child. Part of the time, a stranger was in the room, and part of the time the child was alone.

Ainsworth's observations led her to conclude that there were three patterns in how the babies reacted. Securely attached babies cried when separated, but greeted mother with pleasure when she returned. Ambivalent babies were clingy from the beginning and afraid of the whole situation. They cried profusely at separation, and when mother returned, they sought contact with her but also arched away from her angrily, resisting all efforts at comfort. Avoidant babies seemed independent. They explored the environment freely and barely noticed when mother left the room. On her return, the avoidant baby actually snubbed or avoided her.

In addition to this laboratory observation, Ainsworth's research team had observed each of these infant-mother pairs for seventy-two hours over the prior year. Putting the two together, she concluded that mothers of securely attached children were more responsive to their feeding signals and crying and readily returned their infants' smiles. Mothers of the ambivalent or avoidant babies were inconsistent, unresponsive, or rejecting of their babies.

These patterns of relating and viewing the world persist into adulthood. Parental absence is far from abuse, but the effects on children can be devastating. Dr. Brenda Hunter writes,

> What happens when parents have the capacity to love their children but are absent due to death, divorce, or career demands? For a child, absence does not make the heart grow fonder. Instead, absence generates profound feelings of rejection and a yearning for love that can dominate the whole of life. Harvard psychiatrist Armand Nicholi says that those individuals who suffer from severe nonorganic emotional illness have one thing in common: all have experienced the "absence of a parent through death, divorce, a time demanding job or other reasons." A parent's inaccessibility, either physically, emotionally, or both, "can profoundly influence a child's emotional health."

It matters that a mother is present, both physically and emotionally, during her child's early life. If she is lost in depression, or exhausted by the multiple demands of her life, or absent for long hours each day, her relationship with her child will be affected.[2]

Children need the consistent, available love of their mothers. Without it, they feel unloved and may experience difficulty in intimate relationships for the rest of their lives. On the other hand, researchers have found that securely attached children have more social skills and better coping skills when they reach school age.[3]

I came across this story in a book by Marilee Horton that shows, once again, that the wisdom of children far surpasses that of experts. She says,

> I just heard of a little boy who ran into his house exclaiming, "I just love my house; it is the best house in the whole world."
>
> A neighbor who was visiting said, "Why don't you visit me? My house is just like yours, isn't it? What makes yours different?"
>
> "Well, I don't know, I guess it's Mamma!"[4]

Given all of the above, doesn't your physical and emotional presence seem a small price to pay for the emotional health of your child?

Don't Need Day Care

Attachment theory research seems to say that the stay-at-home role for mothers is best for babies. This research has sparked a great deal of debate and controversy over the issue of day care, a debate we must pay close attention to in order to make the right choice for our children.

"Attachment theory proponents tend to see full-time day care in the first year as a risk, and Jay Belsky, an attachment

researcher at Pennsylvania State University, has voiced the
concern that if you put your baby in substitute care for more
than twenty hours a week, you are running a serious risk of
his becoming anxiously attached—which could skew his
subsequent efforts to relate to the outside world."[5] The basic
thrust of this line of research is the belief that the baby may
feel rejection as a result of the daily separations.

Why hasn't our generation, raised in the era of liberation
and openness, heard about this research? Why aren't we
handed copies of these studies when we go to sign up for
day care? Instead, we are given copies of regulations stating
how many children a worker is allowed to have and how
many items of play equipment are required for a day care
center. Why isn't this information part of the cultural education we receive on having it all and finding fulfillment?

Referring to the work of Belsky and others, Karl Zins-
meister, an adjunct scholar at the American Enterprise Institute, says, "This message has not really gotten into the
women's press in any significant way. It has not really been
presented fairly or well. The real revolution in the scientific
research that has taken place in the last five or ten years is
still kind of secret."[6]

Many of us have been sold the idea that we can combine
a brilliant career with being a wonderful mom. We need to
make a more realistic assessment of this scenario. Zinsmei-
ster continues, "First of all, there's just no evidence that you
can raise children as a hobby on the side and have them come
out right. . . . Second, it's very unfair to the parent to set up
this expectation that they can do these two things at once.
. . . This isn't forever and ever, but for that limited period
of time you have got to be prepared to just focus."[7] If we
take on the job of raising children, we have to be prepared
to "narrow the channel to strengthen the stream."[8]

What about child care in a noninstitutional setting, like
your home? In 1987, research was done on middle class families whose children were cared for in their own homes by

someone other than mom. The researchers observed that when a mother worked full-time outside the home at least during the last four months of her baby's first year of life, the chance that the child would be insecurely attached to mother significantly increased. This insecure attachment is manifested by uncooperative attitudes, and the children tend to be more unpopular than children raised by their mothers.[9]

Author Donna Otto quotes two researchers from the University of Texas who discovered that "children who had been in full-time child care programs during preschool years demonstrated poorer study skills, lower grades, and diminished self-concept in later years." She then passed along the observation of Byrna Seagle, a Stanford University developmental psychologist, who asks, "How much of your life is going to be spent as a mother of a little baby? When you are 60 years old, what are you more likely to remember: the first six months of your child's life, or a case you won?"[10]

Bingo! That hit home for me. While it has been a brief two and a half years since I practiced law full-time, I cannot remember the names of significant clients or their companies. I do, however, remember the last dozen clever things my children said or did.

We don't really know how our choice of full-time work will affect children in the long run. But a look at the current generation of twenty-year-olds is revealing. "One psychologist has said that never before in American history have so many children been raised by strangers."[11] Over 50 percent of these children come from families of divorce. This age group, called Generation X, reports feelings of disillusionment and despair.

One "twentysomething" wrote recently, "So many of us who are in our twenties now were born into homes that had already fallen apart . . . no sense of security and safety, no sense of home at all. So we muddle through our adult lives, wandering around, kind of dazed, kind of wasted, looking like lost children who are still waiting to be claimed at the security office of the shopping mall where our parents last lost track of us." This young writer laments, "At one time, a kid got two parents who did their best to get it right; but now, taking stepparents into account a kid can have twice as many guardians—along with nannies, therapists, tutors and what-not—but somehow, all these people put together can't seem to raise a child decently. It's like having 92 channels of cable and nothing to watch."[12] Nothing to watch, and no one to watch them. One cannot help but wonder how much of their malaise is due to the choices their liberated parents made.

Some would argue that exposure to other adults and children in day care is healthy for a child because it helps make them adequately socialized. However, "All else being equal, having numerous caretakers is not broadening for the young child but is, to a greater or lesser degree, crippling."[13]

Even if you are happy with your day care center and your child seems happy and well adjusted, will staff turnover throw your child for a loop? Keep in mind that, "Day care centers have the highest rate of staff turnover of any human services profession. The reason for the heavy turnover is a combination of low pay, low status, and physical and emotional exhaustion—burn out."[14] I have heard a number of mothers lament the fact that their child attaches to a particular caregiver only to see that person leave for another position. What follows is a heart-rending period of readjustment for their child with each new caregiver.

Another factor to consider in day care centers is the high incidence of illness among the children. Every working mom has faced the panic of waking up to find a child with a high fever on an important day at work. People at work are counting on you; your child is also counting on you. "Illness in children is one of the things that some of the often childless 'professional feminists' never talked about in espousing the notion of 'having it all.'"[15] It puts the working mother in a no-win situation, and that happens for many at least a dozen times a year.

For women who can afford it, a solution to the illness problem is live-in help. But even this seemingly perfect arrangement has its problems. "Even for those who can afford live-in help of full-time nannies, trustworthy child care can be a major worry. Turnover in care givers is high, and the exact delineation of household and child-care chores is often problematic. There is also the added burden of being an employer. One well-to-do suburban mother of two told us that her family went through four care givers in one year and noted that she was getting stress headaches and her child was beginning to cry whenever anybody left the house."[16]

As mentioned earlier, children need quantity time, not just quality time. But you can't give it to them when you're giving 125 percent on the job. Your family ends up at a deficit. Mom Janice Smullen was lucky enough to realize this: "I saw the negative effects of day care centers and felt children were a higher priority than money/career."

From everything the experts have said, the more time you spend with your child, the more likely she will form a healthy attachment to you that will benefit her in all her future relationships. But it takes time, and children need lots of it—not just stolen moments of planned quality time.

On a lighter note, mom Barbara Trudel says, "No one in the world can love our kids as much as my husband and I do. If they drive me to distraction virtually every day, how can I expect someone with no relation to them to put up with their shenanigans without wanting to put them through the nearest wall?"

Mary Pride, an outspoken supporter of mothers at home, laments the fact that, "Our whole society is falling down and worshiping before the shrine of experts . . . Could it be that we mothers are the real experts on mothering?"[17]

You are the expert on what is best for your child. When you follow your heart, where does it lead you?

Sharing the Joys of Childhood

On a good day, life with our small children is joyful. We watch the sunshine make shadows on the floor. We take delight and wonder in any number of small things to observe. It is a great joy to be physically as well as mentally present to share the joy with them. In *How to Really Love Your Child*, author D. Ross Campbell writes, "It is a great opportunity to meet the emotional needs of a child, give him spiritual training and guidance, and do it in an atmosphere which a child will remember."[18] It is a great joy for both you and your child to seize opportunities and share the joys of childhood, but it takes time.

Dr. Brenda Hunter, champion for the emotional attachment of all children, says, "As parents we invariably give our children a legacy of memories—a sense of home or a deep, abiding feeling of homelessness. It is only as we consider our children's well-being a high priority—and are willing to make the essential sacrifices—that we will give them a rich legacy of memories to treasure throughout their lives. In the process we will not only strengthen society but we will affect future generations as well."[19]

When you're too busy or unavailable, you may not be there to answer many of the million questions that pass through your child's mind about life and the world, like, "Mommy, will I still have my voice when I'm in heaven?" or "Mommy, does God look like Santa Claus?" Having the time to respond to these inquiries slowly, thoughtfully, and sensitively is one of the great joys of motherhood. Our children are pondering some deep issues of life as they grow. Don't you want to be there to help them through?

As I write this book, we are awaiting the adoption of our third child. Our children are all excited, and they have lots of questions about life, earth, death, and heaven. For instance, they know that my parents are in heaven with God. They also have heard hundreds of times that children are a great gift from God. Clare put it all together the other day and asked me if my parents were in heaven taking care of the new baby until it was time for her to come and live with us. What if I had been in court trying a case when she made this connection? I would have missed a teachable moment to share my faith and beliefs on life and death.

And children can be so much fun! Some of the greatest joy I have experienced is when I took the time to slow down and enjoy life through the eyes of our children. When your daily schedule is jam-packed with commitments and appointments, you don't have an hour to spend being prince and princess or an afternoon to spend catching butterflies in the backyard. Arlene Cardozo observes, "To my mind, the very best thing about participatory mothering is the sheer fun of it, especially because fun has been in short supply for many women for a long time."[20]

The joy you experience at home with your children will endure throughout their lives and will stretch out into the lives of their children. Take the time to enjoy it!

Vessels for Our Values

Nearly every woman I surveyed spoke of the importance of teaching their children values at home. Marnie Murray said, "My husband and I both believe that children need to be with their mother or father during their early childhood to impart our moral and spiritual values before they go out into the school world." One glance at a newspaper or a TV schedule will show you that the world's values may not be the ones you want your child to adopt. Taking the time to personally teach and model for them while they are young will help them learn discernment when they go out into the world.

Former college teacher Norma Kunda said it well: "I'm convinced it's God's design for the family as well as the most important job I could possibly be doing at this point in my life. I know from experience that everything my children learn from me, and most importantly, the values they learn, have a far greater impact on them and will be remembered far longer than anything 99.9% of my college Spanish students learned in my classes. They catch every little thing. I really cannot conceive of entrusting these precious young lives into the hands of strangers during these critical years of their development."

Our culture is vastly different from what it was even a generation ago. We have seen the spiraling decline of values and the ascension of cynicism. In the last decade of this century, our society faces a host of problems including AIDS, suicide, abuse, and rampant crime. Perhaps coming home to be with your children is more important now than ever.

Denise Wickline recognizes this. She says, "I wanted to take full responsibility for training them. . . . I wanted the children to receive a firm, early foundation for life from home, not an institution."

What is the best way for our children to acquire our values? Psychologist Kevin McDonald says, "Children who have a warm, affectionate relationship with their parents will adopt their parents' values while those who have grown up in conflict-ridden homes subject to a daily barrage of negativism will not."[21] That warm, affectionate relationship is built by spending time with and listening to your child.

What are the values you want to pass on to your child? Once you define your own values, you can determine whether you are conveying them to your children. Some of the most common values are these:

> *Faith.* When people mention values, they are usually talking about their faith. We want our children to grow up loving the Lord. We can help them do this by our example, by exposing them to the Word, and by letting them participate in organized religion.
>
> *Honesty.* Always tell your children (and everyone else!) the truth. Break things down into words they can un-

derstand. For example, we always tell our daughter the truth about her adoption. But we give her information appropriate to her age that she is able to process, and we never, never lie to her. It is also important to let your children see you doing the right thing, even if it is uncomfortable or costs you money.

Loyalty. Let your children know that you and your husband are committed to your marriage, especially after a fight. We tell our kids that everyone fights, but it doesn't mean they don't love each other. Make sure your children know they can depend on you. Also, if you say you will do something with them, like go to the park, *go* even if you're tired. They need to know they can count on you.

Courage. Do your children do things that are difficult, or do they get discouraged? How do they see you react to something you're afraid to do? Teach your children that it is okay to make mistakes or to be afraid; it is *not okay* to give up or not try. When our daughter spilled milk the other day, I heard her say just what I have told her a hundred times: "It's okay. I just made a mistake. No big deal."

Self-discipline. Does your child get every toy she asks for? Does she eat any food she desires? Does he go to bed whenever he wants? While they are young, our children are not in control of these things; we are. We can insure that they approach their desires and appetites with moderation. Set a good example. Give them rules to follow about toys, food, and bedtime.

Respect. The best way to teach respect is to show respect. Your child's thoughts, feelings, and preferences are part of her uniqueness. Show respect for her and she will learn it firsthand.

We hear so much about family values now, but the overuse and misuse of the phrase is sickening. In spite of all the talk about family values, divorce continues to skyrocket, and children are the real victims as parents still desperately seek to find happiness and fulfillment. The choice between the quick fix of divorce or the hard work of toughing it out to salvage a marriage is a question of values. If divorce is avoidable through some hard work, sacrifice, and communication, what is the best choice to make for your child? On the eve of a new century, our children need our guidance and help more than ever. But that requires our presence. They can't be raised properly by proxy.

Benefits to Yourself

Called to Be Mothers

At the age of eighty-nine, the famous child care expert Dr. Spock spoke out in favor of at-home moms in a recent interview: "I think that what is taught to American women, especially with college educations, is that the outside job is the highest challenge. I thing that's all wrong. . . . We ought to be teaching children and demonstrating to children as they grow up that fathers as well as mothers consider child care the most gratifying and most satisfying aspect of life. . . . The job should be of secondary or tertiary importance."[22]

Do you feel like ministry is something you have to do at or for your church? How about author Donna Otto's perspective: She says, "As a stay-at-home mom, your ministry is motherhood. You are the one God has called to mother your children. How important it is that you faithfully and joyfully do the job God has called you to do, keeping your eyes on Him and not others."[23]

I first became a mother not by biological surprise, but by true choice. Our children were prayed for and are blissful examples of the grace of a loving God. Even though it seemed like I would never know the joy of motherhood, he loved us enough to entrust our children to our care. Because he has called me to be a mother, I want to do the best job I can to present my children to him with hearts full of love for him. For me, that means taking time at this point in my life to pursue my calling full-time.

In speaking of her calling to motherhood, author Marilee Horton says, "I was called by God to be woman. My limitations are mundane, not glamorous or noble, something a scullery maid could do. But in God's perspective, in the overall plan of things, what I am doing is noble. It is accepting the gift and using it until he places another in my hand."[24]

And this calling is not just to our own children. Debbie Wilcoxen says, "I see my mission field in my backyard and basement." Those of us who are blessed with stable homes can not only be the best mothers of our own children, we can also make room in our hearts for the children of the tired parents down the block. We can keep a watchful eye out for the safety of the neighborhood children. We can provide a homemade snack for a little visitor. We can provide an atmosphere in our homes that makes everyone feel welcomed.

If it is our calling to be mothers, let's do it wholeheartedly and delight in the simple joys of the job.

> *What do you enjoy most about being home?*
>
> *Having time to do the little things that are so fulfilling.*
> —*Denise Wickline*

Putting Family First

No one is suggesting that stay-at-home mothering *must* be a lifelong commitment. If we choose to have children, however, we need to set aside some of our other interests for their benefit while they need us so much.

Dr. Armand M. Nicholi, Jr. serves at Harvard Medical School and Massachusetts General Hospital and has written a great deal about mothers and children. He is quoted in Donna Otto's book, *The Stay-at-Home Mom,* saying, "We need a radical change in our thinking about family. We need a society where people have the freedom to be whatever they choose—but if they choose to have children, then those children must be given the highest priority."[25]

If you want to be good at something, you can't pursue it and three or four other dreams at the same time. There are simply not enough hours in the day. I believe that if we want to be good mothers and give our children the focused attention they need, we must constantly evaluate our other commitments in the light of our highest commitment—the well-being of our children.

When I came home, there was a brief time when I thought I could do a little bit of everything I wanted to do. I was taking some referral cases, doing an occasional arbitration hearing, and pursuing a fairly regular schedule of writing. I thought with this arrangement that I was meeting all my needs for stimulation outside of the home. Yet my schedule was so unpredictable, I often had to scramble to find someone to watch the kids on short notice.

Author Pamela Piljac notes, "And it's always easier to leave your options open . . . to have a little bit of everything rather than taking a chance and making a mistake. Yet, if you try to be everything that you believe you must be, you may discover that your life is without focus, direction, or a true sense of your inner needs."[26]

When I tried to be everything I wanted to be, my experience at home was disjointed and without focus. I realized that I had to set aside the nonessentials to be the best that I could be at the most important things.

"What is central is that we fit the demands of our work around the needs of our families and not that we mortgage our children's emotional health for a career," Dr. Hunter reminds us.[27] The victories and the ego gratification I experienced in the courtroom pale in comparison to the satisfaction I feel when I look at our happy, fairly well-adjusted children. Many a mother has noted that children won't wait to grow up until the tax season is over, until their caseload lessens, or until a pet project is completed. In fact, the time passes so quickly that children seem to grow up in the twinkling of an eye.

Author Pamela Piljac treasures this time of growth. She says, "As a homemaker you have time to grow morally, intellectually, and spiritually. You can savor the experiences that make life enjoyable and create new options for satisfaction and fulfillment. Use your abilities to improve the lives of those around you. Make your home an example of love, nurture, and care. Teach your children to value people over material things. True success is living your life the best way that you can."[28]

In the meantime, there is time to make our house a home. There is time for my spiritual growth as well as planting the seeds for the spiritual growth of our children. Isn't that what it's all about?

Stop Trying to Have It All

Would you live all of your life with all its seasons in five years' time? Probably not. Yet we have been led to believe that we can and should have marriage, career, children, and the prime time of our life simultaneously. Author and mom Christine Davidson explains, "It also did not occur to me that when a woman 'has it all' she has to *handle it all*. To those who still insist that we can have it all I now say, Yes, indeed, all of it: an early heart attack, midnight laundry loads, and weekend catch-up headaches. There is nothing fulfilling about fatigue."[29]

I resigned as superwoman a long time ago. I was just too tired. "Recent research indicates that working women with children put in the equivalent of an entire second shift at home—a shift that comprises most of the child care and household chores," note authors Darcie Sanders and Martha Bullen, referring to the work of Arlie Hochschild, *The Second Shift* (New York: Viking Penguin, 1989).[30] Many women in that position are not only physically exhausted, but also bitter and resentful.

How much better it is to enjoy one day at a time and realize that "We can have it all—but not all at once. And if we live each day fully, we won't have to look back over the terrain of our lives with emotional pain because we were inaccessible to our families while our children were at home. Instead, we will feel blessed as we watch our children leave home, marry, and start their own families."[31]

Rabbi Harold Kushner wrote an article called "The Biggest Mistake I Ever Made" in which he says, "But if I could change anything, it would be those years when I focused on my work and ignored the needs of my wife and young children."[32] He realized he was investing his soul in his work, and not even the death of his son at the tender age of fourteen caused a change in his attitude. Rather, his attitude changed as he himself grew older. At the age of fifty he realized that his wife was right.

Personal Growth

A season of full-time parenting can be a period of great personal growth. "Impossible as it may seem," author Donna Otto says, "there is always time in your day to do the things your heart desires. Every day holds minutes or hours for prayer, Bible study, and reflection."[33] "Indeed, opportunities for personal growth may be the best kept secret about staying home," note the authors of *Staying Home: From Full-Time Professional to Full-Time Parent.*[34] They suggest viewing our time at home as a parenting sabbatical to be used for personal enrichment and learning.

When our two children were very small, I was up to my elbows in diapers and bottles. Because they were seventeen months apart and the second was a high-need baby, I sometimes wondered if I would ever have an unfettered moment with enough energy to have another creative thought. But that time passed, and I have renewed some passionate interests I didn't have time to develop while chasing my career goals. The time I have to pursue them is short, but I am blowing the dust off of some old skills and interests, and I'm having a ball! Dr. Hunter calls the years at home raising children, "the summer of her life"[35] and encourages us to make the most of this time, whether our passion is pottery, politics, art, or aerobics.

What have you been longing to do, but just haven't had the time or emotional energy to pursue? Many women find that taking classes for enrichment or to complete a degree fits in nicely with a season at home. Others take an intense interest in crafts or other domestic arts. Still others start a home-based business, expanding it as the needs of their family change.

Do you want your children to be creative? If you are excited about life and are always learning something new, your children will "catch" your enthusiasm for creativity. By continuing to grow in your own interests, your children will see that the world is indeed an exciting place where they can experiment creatively.

Grow with your children. Don't just stagnate and shuffle into the next season. By nourishing your creative growth, you can burst ahead with life.

Learning to Live in the Present

When I came home to raise our children, one of the first things I did was put away my watch. I didn't have to be bound by schedules and appointments unless they were absolutely necessary. In *The Hurried Child: Growing Up Too Fast Too Soon*,

David Elkind says, "If we concentrate on the here and now, without worrying about yesterday or tomorrow, our children will do likewise . . . The art of living is the most difficult task children have to learn, and they do this best if their parents or caretakers have a way of looking at life as a whole."[36]

Many people today are longing for older times—perhaps because life was simpler then. People didn't have to choose from a hundred brands of cereal at the grocery store. They didn't have to choose from the myriad of activities and opportunities available to us and our children. In their simple lives, they seemed to have more time for people.

But we have to deal with a world that is more complex. In his booklet *The Tyranny of the Urgent*, Charles E. Hummel cautions us against letting the urgent demands of modern life crowd out the really important things. The urgent things are work that never seems finished, a phone that constantly rings, and the many requests for "just a little" of your time. The author unequivocally states that, "Freedom from the tyranny of the urgent is found in the example and promise of our Lord." Prayerfully waiting on God, perhaps in a quiet time of meditation and prayer, is the only real way to combat the tyranny of the urgent. "If we continue in the word of our Lord, we are truly his disciples. And he will free us from the tyranny of the urgent, free us to do the important, which is the will of God."[37]

While I was still working, it seemed I was always living in some time other than the present. When I was at work, I worried about the children. When I was home, I worried about clients. Since I have been home, I have been practicing living in the present and have never felt more content and peaceful.

Jana Trovato says that what she enjoys most about being home is the fact that she is "able to be more single-minded in caring for my family." She can really be there when her mind and her heart aren't torn in a dozen different directions. Cindy McCabe says, "I need this time at home, physically and emotionally, and my rewards are my health; a healthy, happy, and confident daughter who is an endless source of surprise, delight, and pride; and a stronger, happier, and more relaxed marriage." All this takes time and emotional energy.

An interesting perspective on time is presented by Dr. Richard Swensen in his book *Margin*. He notes that time was God's way of making sure everything didn't happen at once. One antidote to the hurry sickness we have in our society is to offer this question to God each day: "What do you want me to do with this time today?"[38] Perhaps the answer to that question will be that he wants you to enjoy the new spring daffodils with your children. Do you have the time?

Making Peace with Your Past

Bearing and raising children inevitably brings up memories and thoughts from one's own childhood. If those memories are happy and secure, the new mother will not feel conflict in her new role. But what about the mother who lacked mothering? It is possible to give our children what we did not have. And in the process of loving and nurturing them, we can heal some of the wounds from our past.

Dr. Brenda Hunter observes, "A new mother has a wonderful challenge: she has a reason (in the person of her new baby) to confront her unnurtured past and grow as a person. Many women have done just this, and their lives are richer for it."[39]

In reviewing the research in this area, Dr. Hunter notes that, "Attachment patterns get passed on cross-generationally. A daughter who has experienced maternal rejection may have difficulty creating a secure attachment relationship with her own child." However, mothers who had worked through the pain of their own childhoods to forgiveness and healing had securely attached children.[40] Our incentive to find that healing is the love we feel for our own children and our desire to be better parents to them.

Like so many women today, my childhood was not ideal. I was the daughter of a severely depressed mother. I never resolved my relationships with my parents because they died when I was a teenager. So I carried this baggage with me when I became a mother. It took me years to realize that I would not necessarily become my mother. And I also had to forgive my parents for dying when I was so young. It took a long time to do, but with much prayer and introspection, I came to a place of peace about my parents. Becoming a mother, especially a mother of daughters, encouraged me to confront the bitterness and sadness in my own heart and to prayerfully let it go so it would not poison the hearts of our daughters. Instead, I think I have brought richness and depth to my mothering by incorporating some of the positive attributes of both my parents. I can say with Dr. Hunter, "Home became a place of healing once I stopped running, owned the pain, and confronted the past with all its wrack and ruin. Home can be a place of healing for you, too, when the former desolations of the spirit are repaired."[41]

You can pray for the healing of your past. Start with the psalms. Make this your prayer to God: "Search me, O God, and know my heart; test me and know my anxious thoughts" (Ps. 139:23). God knows your past and the hurts you have suffered. They *can* be healed, and God can help you to find wholeness. Turn them over to him, and ask him to help you grow to be a healthy, healed mother to your children. I have prayed for and found a measure of healing and rest, but our daughters have been the real benefactors.

Benefits to Your Marriage

Cohesion

About a year into my adventure at home, I felt my marriage was drifting. I put so much energy into our children that I confess I neglected my marriage. My husband and I made all of the mistakes that couples are cautioned against. We didn't schedule time together, sometimes harbored resentments, didn't talk, and didn't listen.

It took lots of healing time together, prayer, and talk to put our marriage back on a firm footing. But now we have a unity that probably would not have been possible without my commitment to full-time mothering. Now we are each less stressed out and have more time for each other. Sometimes it doesn't feel that way, but at the end of a bad day, I like to reflect on how many more burdens on our shoulders we would have had at the end of the day if we had not made our lifestyle change. Then I can count my blessings again.

Denise Wickline says, "My husband really enjoys me being there and I could tell that it is very calming and stabilizing for him. It benefits the entire family for me to be home. When I think about it, I don't know if what I would have left over to give them after a day outside the home would be of much value. I'd rather give them my best than the scraps. They're worth that much to me."

Mary Hotwagner, another mom at home, sees another benefit for her husband: "When I am with the children, he is always made aware of what the girls are doing, what needs they have during the day when he's away, and they are always aware of how much their dad cares for them." Can our children get that from another caregiver? Even though we are the ones at home with them all day, we can foster the relationship between father and children.

We have found a renewed cohesion to our relationship. In addition to our growth in closeness as a family, we have experienced a spiritual renewal, both individually and as a couple. I don't know if this would have happened if we had continued our individual career agendas. I weep with sadness and gratitude when I think of how I almost threw all of this away for the sake of my ego gratification and career advancement—sadness because of my unfairness to my husband and gratitude that our faith saw us through.

Nurturing Your Husband

I made an amazing discovery when I came home to raise our children. My husband became a better father and a better partner to me. Of course, it took me about a year to realize that I was less stressed, happier, and more cheerful with him, which had a positive impact. The fact is that our husbands also need our nurturing and attention. But we are ill equipped to meet his needs, the needs of our children, *and* the needs of clients and customers, especially when they are all needy at the same time.

Our husbands need us to affirm them spiritually as well. Let him know that you respect the fact that he is God's man. If you are not feeling respectful of your husband, remind yourself that he is deserving of your respect because of his status as a child of God.

There was an unspoken resentment in our relationship when I was working. There was a subtle scorekeeping of who had changed the most diapers or done the most chores. Now because we are less stressed and more focused, we do things for one another out of love and compassion, not as scheduled obligations.

When there is a relaxed, warm atmosphere in your home, many of the petty annoyances of domestic life are tamed. Love can grow more freely and endure for the long haul.

*What do you enjoy least about
being home?*

*The days are too short. At times I desire
outside affirmation, but that usually occurs
when I've lost my perspective.*
—Denise Wickline

Living All the Days of Our Lives

In her classic work, *Creative Counterpart,* Linda Dillow talks about a friend of hers who took to heart the words of Psalm 90:12—"Teach us to number our days aright, that we may gain a heart of wisdom"—and totaled up the number of days she would have left if she lived to be seventy. This thirty-year-old figured she had 14,600 days left on earth.[42] How will you spend the days you have left? When you reach the end, will you look back with the peace of contentment or with regret for not having taken the time to live those days to their fullest?

Denise Wickline feels passionately about this. She says, "This is such a special time of life—I want to enjoy every moment of it and not waste it away by poor planning, complaining, or misplaced priorities. Nothing in this world is so precious as my God and the family he's given me, nor is anything else going to last into eternity as they are. My relationships at home are the recipients of my energy, time, and love. I am secure enough in God's estimation of my worth that I can serve them wholeheartedly, with much satisfaction, regardless of current social philosophy. What a tremendous freedom to love and to be of value where it matters!"

I urge you to find in favor of a quiet life at home, raising the children God has blessed you with. As you retire to consider your verdict, remember that your children as well as your husband need *you,* and that you can make a difference in their lives by devoting this time to them.

3

Can You Afford to Stay Home?

One of the first steps in deciding whether to take the leap from being a working mom to being a stay-at-home mom is to figure the financial cost of each option. For some of you, especially those with more than one child, the question might be, "Can you afford to work?" rather than "Can you afford to stay home?" Specific suggestions on how to live within your means are discussed in chapter 11, but you'll first have to make the decision to take the initial plunge.

What's a Mom Worth?

For the book *The Stay-at-Home Mom*, Donna Otto had C.P.A. Nicholas Pichione calculate what a mom is worth. "The worth of her services totals $699 per week or $36,348 per year."[1] Whew! Using information from financial analyst Sylvia Porter, Dr. Brenda Hunter notes, "Porter found the labor performed by a mother at home would cost a family $23,580 in Greensboro, $26,962 in Los Angeles, $27,538 in New York, and $28,735 in Chicago . . . In a sense, even this analysis is demeaning to the mother at home because Porter only looked at relatively menial duties. She did not consider some of the higher-status jobs every mother at home performs: coach, teacher, interior decorator, religious education instructor, and child psychologist, to name a few."[2]

If you think the staying home option is only for women whose husbands have high-paying jobs, consider these words from Arlene Rossen Cardozo, the author of the groundbreaking book, *Sequencing*:

> When I first began researching *Sequencing*, I assumed that the woman's decision to leave her career would be positively correlated with her husband's income—that the more he earned, the more she would be likely, if she wanted to leave her work, to do so. And I assumed that, correspondingly, the less he earned, the less inclined she would be to leave. But this is not always the case. Husband's income and wife's sequencing do not necessarily go hand in hand.[3]

The author defines sequencing as looking at one's life as a series of three stages:

> Stage one, the full-time career; stage two, full-time mothering; and stage three, reincorporating a career in new ways so that family and profession complement rather than conflict.[4]

"Careful planning is necessary," notes author Mary Ann Cahill. "The first step lies in taking a stand against the all-too-prevalent thinking that added income will solve all of a family's problems. If this added income means separation of mother and baby, then it may not be the solution; it may be a new source of stress. The long-range effects of separation are seldom as easy to correct as a temporary shortage of funds."[5] Are there some other assets you can tap into to buy yourself some time at home? Is there a retirement fund you can cash in, or a money market fund stashed away, or an insurance policy you can borrow against or cash in? Other women have sold jewelry, musical instruments, or boats. Keep in mind that these precious items can all be replaced when your cash situation improves, but you can't replace your children's childhoods.

So, how tight will your cash situation be? When you sit down to do the cost analysis below, calculate the actual dollar figure you will be ahead by working. Then average out the number of hours you work, and decide if that is really the highest and best use of your time.

Spending Analysis

Let's take a look at the numbers that might be involved in your financial jump. Whether you're counting calories or counting pennies, there is no substitute for writing everything down so you can accurately assess a situation. Mary Hotwager says, "A strict budget followed by both of us made us aware that we could make it with one salary." But you both have to be committed to examining and paring down your lifestyle and spending habits.

To begin your analysis, write down all your expenses—the necessities as well as the niceties—starting with your house payment. Here's a worksheet for you to use.

Current Monthly Budget

Mortgage or rent _____
(include principle, taxes, and interest and make a note of your current interest rate)
Utilities
    gas _____
    electric _____
    water/sewer _____

phone _____

cable _____

Credit payments

car loan(s) _____

credit card(s) _____

other loan(s) _____

Home maintenance _____

Insurance premiums

(monthly average)

health _____

life _____

auto _____

homeowners or rental _____

(if not included above)

dental _____

other _____

Food

weekly grocery average _____

dining out related to work _____

(include coffee, snacks,

convenience items for work)

Discount store items

diapers and baby items _____

toiletries _____

cosmetics _____

Clothing

children _____

husband _____

your everyday clothes _____

your work clothes _____

Haircuts _____

Dry cleaning

routine _____

specifically for your job _____

Laundry _____

Professional expenses _____
(dues, etc.)
Fuel/car maintenance
    routine _____
    specifically related to your job _____
Parking
    routine _____
    specifically related to your job _____
Train/bus fares for work _____
(if applicable, his and hers)
Furniture and household decor _____
Savings _____
Regular investments _____
Entertainment
    movie rental or theater _____
    baby-sitting _____
    dining out _____
    health clubs _____
    classes _____
    other _____
Vacation _____
(divide by twelve)
Books, subscriptions, music _____
Children's books and toys _____
Child care _____
Charitable contributions _____
Church contributions or tithes _____
Household help _____
Gifts _____
Other _____

Total monthly expenses _____
Total expenses related to work
(and other discretionary expenses) _____
Estimated monthly budget for stay-at-home mom _____

After you have everything in black and white, calculate a monthly total. It may take you a few weeks to get a realistic financial picture. It is also a good idea for you and your husband to each fill out one of these budgets and then compare your estimates on some of the discretionary spending. Couples often differ in their perceptions of these things.

Then take a highlighter pen and highlight the expenses specifically related to your work and any discretionary expenses you would be willing to forego in order to stay home. Add these highlighted expenses and subtract them from your total for an estimated monthly budget for your family with you as an at-home mom.

The Cost of Your Job

The monetary costs of a second income may not be worth the benefit. In mid 1992, the *Wall Street Journal* reported the extent to which job costs eat up second paychecks. They said, "Two earner families lose up to two-thirds of the second paycheck to work-related costs, a study of Labor Department consumer-spending data shows." For middle income families, child care, household help, clothing, food away from home, transportation, and other work-related costs eat up 56 percent of the second paycheck. In lower income families, the figure is 46 percent. For upper income families, it's 68 percent.[6]

Your income probably puts your family in a higher tax bracket. Check to see if you are taking the maximum allowable exemptions on your husband's W-2 forms at work. Then use this year's tax table to estimate next year's taxes on one income. This will give you a realistic picture of your husband's take-home income.

The extra costs of clothing, dining out, and work-related transportation can be slashed from your budget (personally,

I was relieved to get out of panty hose!), but your largest monetary savings will undoubtedly be child care. Darcie Sanders and Martha Bullen note, "One rule of thumb is that you need to make roughly two and a half times your child care costs for working outside the home to be economically advantageous."[7] Let's see what that looks like in numbers.

> *W*hat do you enjoy most about being home?
>
> *Being there when my kids need me.*
> —*Karen Gresk*

With an infant and toddler in Du Page County, Illinois, the average cost was $150 per week for our infant and $120 per week for our toddler. Undoubtedly these figures will vary across the country, but they are representative of rates in metropolitan suburban areas. Our weekly child care bill would have been $270 per week or $1,215 per month. Having had a godly day care provider, I know that it is difficult to put a price on quality care. In fact, I often told our former provider that she undercharged me and that her services were worth far more. But my *take home* pay, according to this formula, would have to exceed $675 per week or $3,037.50 per month. Add to these figures the other work-related expenses and the amount is staggering.

Barbara Trudel of Rhode Island says, "I am, in fact, saving the family money. Since the cost of child care for three kids ages three, one, and seven months is so high, I'd be spending the majority of my pay on it."

Because we bought the cheapest house we could find and kept some old cars running for a while, we actually improved our financial situation, even though the total dollar value of our income declined. Amazing? Not really, especially after you calculate the cost of working and the tax savings to be gained by being a one-income family.

A Simpler Lifestyle

During the years I struggled through law school (both paying for it and surviving it), I always assumed I would make a lot of money, live in a nice house, drive a nice car, and take nice vacations. When children jumped into the equation and we contemplated raising a family on a police officer's salary, we had to modify some of those expectations. I complained a little about having to make cutbacks and sacrifices for a short time after coming home. I missed the no-holds-barred trips to the mall where I could buy what I wanted or thought I needed. I missed the discretionary income I had as a DINK (double income, no kids). But we were convinced that the best lifestyle choice for us that would be rewarding now and have eternal significance was to put our children first. This choice meant that our children would not have the nicest clothes, the newest toys, and the satisfaction of their every whim. In fact, we almost go to the other extreme to try to insure that they don't turn into suburban brats. It also means that we have to weekly or sometimes daily examine our choices and priorities.

One of the resources that really helped us to get our financial priorities straight was a book by Dr. Richard A. Swenson called *Margin: How to Create the Emotional, Physical, Financial & Time Reserves You Need*. He says margin "is having breath left at the top of the staircase, money left at the end of the month, and sanity left at the end of adolescence."[8] His book is a thought-provoking, moving analysis of the price we all pay for progress—and for many of us the price is pain. His prescription for the malady of being marginless in our finances includes decreasing spending, increasing income, and increasing savings—just as any good financial advisor would advise. But Dr. Swenson also encourages readers to examine the spiritual aspects of our relationship to money, such as learning to live within our harvest. Contentment and simplicity won't be far behind.

The word "sacrifice" is not in the vocabulary of some families. But it was a part of Denise Wickline's family even before she came home: "We were already living below our means, so the transition was a little smoother." But for others, like Marnie Murray's, the husband picks up the slack: "He does lots of overtime and frequently works fourteen to sixteen hour days."

Author Christine Davidson agonized over the working-mom versus stay-at-home mom dilemma herself. She notes that, "Those of us who suffer conflicts about being working mothers often say, 'But I *have* to work.' Often this statement should be amended to, 'I have to work to maintain our standard of living.' It is difficult for women of my generation to do without, to lower our sights, and to recognize that there is a difference between what it is *nice* to have and what is *necessary* to have."[9]

It may be nice to have a comfortable material life, but I believe it is not only necessary, but crucial that we take our responsibility to our children seriously and wholeheartedly. A former college instructor, Dr. Norma Kunda, says, "Certainly we could have and do more 'things' if I were receiving additional earnings, but it's really only a matter of adjusting our expectations, budget, and standard of living so they're in line with one income. It's a matter of priorities. Also, the Lord has been blessing our attempts to obey what we believe is his will by providing for our needs."

If your heart yearns to be home full-time with your children, maybe you need to take a leap of faith and come home. Mary Ann Cahill says that taking the step, "is like going off the high dive in swimming for the first time. The only way to do it is simply to let go. Take a deep breath and jump."[10]

Home Is Where You Can Afford the Mortgage

If you are considering purchasing a new house or scaling down to a smaller one, consider this: "More young mothers get caught on a treadmill of working because of high monthly mortgage payments than because of anything else. . . . High mortgage payments are the number one nemesis of stay-at-home mothers, so consider a home purchase carefully or wait a few years."[11]

Our house is small—and I mean small! It took me a while to appreciate it, but with lots of paint, some curtains, and other personal touches, I fell in love with it. Most of all, I love the fact that we can afford it, and we don't sweat our mortgage payments. Our kids will not remember a cramped house. But they will remember the time, attention, and love that was there.

Nancy V. recalls, "My husband and I knew that having me quit my job to stay home and raise our child would mean making financial sacrifices, so we deliberately bought a small house that we knew we could afford with one income."

Another factor to consider if you plan to stay in your current home is the possibility of refinancing your mortgage. The financial rule of thumb is that when rates drop at least two percentage points below the rate you currently pay, your mortgage is worth refinancing. Anything less than 2 percent would probably be eaten up in fees and closing costs. But lenders vary widely in the deals they will offer. Call to get estimates from at least three lenders, do the math, and decide if you can save substantially on your monthly mortgage payment.

Amusing Ourselves to Debt

You and your husband may differ on this subject, but you need to carefully examine your entertainment budget. Paring this down to a bare minimum (while enjoying some free family-friendly activities discussed elsewhere in this book) is worth serious consideration.

> *What do you enjoy least about being home?*
>
> *The lack of adult conversation and bad days when kids are all stir crazy.*
>
> —Karen Gresk

An expenditure to cut might be a health club membership. There are cheaper ways to stay fit. And then there are the movies. For our family, a trip to the movie theater costs about twenty dollars. If we buy goodies, we add at least another ten dollars. If we leave the kids at home, the admission cost is lower, but the cost of baby-sitting really bumps up the total. However, we can rent a movie for two dollars and make our own goodies for a much cheaper family movie night. Also, we rarely go out to eat, and when we do it is usually with a two-for-one special or other coupon.

There is so much you can do with your family that is free or low cost. Be a little creative! Modify some of your entertainment to make it cost effective. Make it a challenge to see if you can have fun without spending gobs of money. Simple things are the best, and you will not be setting your children up to expect to have experienced everything out of life by the age of ten.

Another mom, writing in *The Heart Has Its Own Reasons,* notes, "There's no need for bigger, better, brighter, whiter, faster, and shinier. But there is a need for simpler, smaller, slower, and saner."[12]

Final Considerations

One final suggestion comes from financial writer Anita Jones-Lee who suggests that you try to "rent the lifestyle" before committing to quit your job.[13] Try to arrange a leave of absence from your job to sample life at home—both from a financial as well as an emotional perspective. For some couples, reality can come as a surprise. Debbi Heinze notes, "We had banked my money for our house and our car, so we never really lived on two incomes, but six months after I quit consulting, boom! We were paycheck to paycheck."

As you contemplate this season and the possible sacrifices you may have to make, keep in mind that it doesn't have to be forever. At some point in the lives of your children, you may decide to go back to work at least part-time to supplement the family income. You don't have to look ahead to years and years of scarcity, because your children will grow and your opportunities to contribute to your family will change and expand. This short season at home could be just a fraction of your time on the planet. Surely another season with other challenges will follow.

You have heard the old story—the man on his deathbed was not wishing he could have spent more time at the office—he was wishing he could have cherished his family time more. That really hit home for me with each new case I took shortly before I quit. When our children are grown, will I be telling myself, "Gee, I wish I had handled more cases, sued more people, and spent more time in court"? I don't think so! I am constantly grateful I realized this early in our children's lives.

The last "cost" for you to consider is not financial. "Another word for these job-related expenses without price tags is stress," notes Mary Ann Cahill. If you're being torn in too many different directions, surely your family will suffer. "A mother must make a decision about who deserves the first call on her time. If she decides her baby—her family—deserve not just a small portion of her time, but a large quantity of quality time, then she knows what she must choose."[14]

As you struggle with this decision, consider that perhaps you are dealing with the issue of trust. "With all the wisdom that God promises to supply us with to make the best use of our money and talents, we must not forget that what HE is mainly trying to teach us is to trust in Him."[15]

Can you trust him to show you the way to a season at home? How much is the opportunity to get to know your kids worth to you? Where will working get you?

There is a story circulating in our area about a private school near a train station. The janitor was letting the kids into the building at 7 A.M. because their parents would drop the kids off that early so they could catch the train downtown to work. The kids became too much for him to handle, so he had to quit opening the building early.

These parents undoubtedly felt they were doing the best for their kids by footing the bill for a private education. But what are the kids learning about their value to their parents when they are dropped off daily like dry cleaning and collected at the end of the day that the paid experts have spent with them?

No thanks. I'll take care of ours myself.

4

❧

Making the Psychological Transformation

When I was in high school and college, it was important to me to display my identity to the world. In high school I had notebooks with names and sayings scrawled on them. In college, I wore t-shirts or put stickers on books and cars to denote my interests or affiliations. In law school, I wore the label of law student proudly. I was training to be an attorney—a calling that seemed awfully important at the time.

The actual practice of law was ego bruising for a few years. You discover that you learned nothing in law school and that your actual education begins when school ends. The real ego-gratification came a few years into practice. Before becoming a mother at home, I enjoyed a good professional reputation in a small town. I loved having people call me ma'am; schmoozing with judges, politicians, and other lawyers; and being referred to as counselor.

Then the children came and a major move shortly after. Our children, our marriage, and my sanity were strained to the max. A minor accident at the end of an eighty-mile commute on a rainy night (my fault due to fatigue and stress) made me ask myself, "Why am I doing this?" I don't profess to be a superwoman. Reality for me is that I cannot do a good job mothering and lawyering at the same time. I made the decision that night to stay home, and I had the dent in my front fender to remind me each day of the gravity of that decision.

Changing Your Identity

I was shocked to wake up one morning and discover that I was a suburban housewife. Hardly anyone here knows I'm a lawyer; I rarely wear t-shirts with writing on them; and my bumper is sticker free. But for the first time in my life I feel peaceful and free.

A similar experience was shared by Denise Wickline, another mom at home. She said, "I experienced an unexpected clinging to my identity as a teacher for a while, especially when I filled out forms asking what my occupation was. Also, I winced for a while when grocery clerks asked for my business phone. It didn't take very long, though, to feel secure saying 'homemaker.'"

Our children have helped me rethink my identity. They have taught me to slow down, listen to them and myself, learn who they are, and re-learn who I am. They have taught me that it is more important to *be* than to *have*, more important to *enjoy* than to *achieve*, and that success does not always wear tailored suits and panty hose.

Our children have also taught me that being a mother is hard work. Cindy McCabe says, "Anyone who has done both will tell you staying home with children is harder than working at an office. Most of my neighbors work at least part-time to maintain their identity and earn money. They encourage me to get a job because they know I am very achievement oriented, but right now that isn't the answer.

I need to learn to be happy without 'work' or how will I survive retirement? I also believe parenting is very valuable work, although it is unpleasant sometimes."

Many women of my generation (I am climbing the hill towards forty) have created their definition of career and life success from the male definition. Debbi Heinze says, "I loved working; it was how I defined myself." In our quest to be liberated and equal, we cast aside some of our important roles and most crucial responsibilities. We took equal standing in society to mean that our roles also had to be the same, and in so doing cheated ourselves out of some of the greatest joys of being a woman. Men and women are as different as night and day. God created us differently so we could complement one another. Instead of women trying to follow the male definition of success, why can't we enjoy and celebrate that diversity?

Arlene Cardozo notes that, "Feelings of identity loss affect a woman who leaves her job in direct proportion to the degree to which she has accepted the male careerism norm. Therefore, women who felt a high degree of conflict in the first place are the hardest hit. When a woman's entire being is tied up with her occupation and then she leaves her job, she cannot help but suffer feelings of loss, anxiety, and even grief. These are the same feelings experienced by the man who, at retirement, finds himself bereft because he has been his occupation and now feels that without his job he's without a self."[1]

I have reevaluated my definition of success and in so doing have discovered that I was not always totally comfortable following my former path to success. My need to achieve and impress came from trying to fit a definition of success that didn't always fit *me*. As the mother of daughters, I hope I can give them a legacy of freedom to choose their own definitions of success, rather than merely fulfilling cultural expectations. I want them to have true freedom of choice.

Author Mary Ann Cahill comments that, "Mothering is the original one-day-at-a-time job. Mothers, as well as their children, need time in which to grow."[2] Returning home caused me to rebuild a self. When I could no longer say I was a lawyer, I really didn't know who I was because I had not searched for and developed other aspects of myself. I had so strongly defined myself by work-related tasks that coming home to raise our children was truly a shock to me.

But being a mother at home has taught me to embrace the parts of myself that are *beyond* just being a lawyer or a mother at home. I am discovering new interests and rekindling old ones I had abandoned. And along the way I am liking the person I have become over the years more and more because I am learning to honor the past, relish the present, and be excited about the future. When conflicts with the past and fears about the future are resolved and not allowed to poison the day-to-day life of a mother, she can be surprisingly satisfied. Jackie Wellwood, mom, says, "Motherhood was more satisfying than even the best of jobs that I had."

In her research for the book *Sequencing*, Arlene Cardozo found certain factors that differentiate women who are happy at home from those who are not. The first factor is "a very clear sense of who she is and why she is at home raising her family."[3] For some women, this conviction seems to occur at conception. For the rest of us, it may take some time to figure out.

It may be helpful for you to write out your answers to the question, "Why do I want to stay home?" If you are home raising your children in order to nurture them, give them solid values, and make them feel secure and loved, then your "job description" would not be limited to housewife and cook. Rather, you are a nurturer, value preserver, security provider, and lover of your children.

It can be brutal to compare yourself to other mothers. You may feel that others are doing a better job. You may resent the mother down the street who always has time to bake the cookies and supervise twenty kids in the yard for soda and snacks. But you can be the best mom that you can be to your children. That relationship is what is most important. Ultimately, your identity should rest in your relationship to Christ and your importance to your family.

"Don't compare yourself to anyone," says Donna Otto. "Don't worry about your identity now that you are a stay-at-home mom. You are a child of God, and He can use everything you are to minister to Him and to your family. Rest in your identity in Christ."[4]

As you ponder the question of a new identity, remember that your true identity is in Jesus Christ and that will never change. Donna Otto comments, "You haven't lost your identity; you've simply moved it! Your gifts and abilities have been relocated to a new arena. . . . You need a director, someone who knows you and can help you understand how your unique gifts and abilities can be applied at home. That director, of course, is Jesus."[5] Always remember, "Just as you received Christ Jesus as Lord, continue to live in him, rooted and built up in him, strengthened in the faith as you were taught, and overflowing with thankfulness" (Col. 2:6–7). That identity remains constant, whether you are a corporate executive, a scullery maid, or a mother at home.

Once the transition is made, however, "many women say they become much more secure of themselves than they have previously been. For they can recognize themselves as individuals over and apart from the work they are trained to perform or the particular place they held in their fields."[6]

If you are a Christian woman who hasn't already done so, this may be a time to discover your true identity in Christ. While nurturing your children, you can nurture your relationship with Jesus.

Feeling Unprepared

There were so many things I was unprepared for—unending housework and laundry, lack of sleep, and loss of identity. I don't think any class or parenting text can prepare a woman for the work of mothering. Each day holds new experiences and challenges.

Some days I felt invisible. The children would cry, and I couldn't comfort them. I would talk to my husband, and he wouldn't be hearing anything I said. But it got better . . . with time and faith in God, most things do.

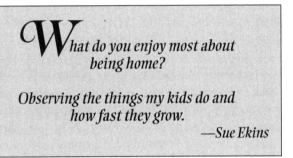

What do you enjoy most about being home?

Observing the things my kids do and how fast they grow.

—Sue Ekins

I also gained a lot of weight. I've never been slim, but I packed on quite a few pounds with my pregnancy. After delivering the baby and all the major upheavals that came after that, I actually gained more weight.

"Lost your baby weight yet?" someone would say.

"Nope. I just added more to it," I'd reply. In my family, we like to joke that we have a rapid holiday weight gain contest, and I usually win.

So there I was in my sweatpants, carrying lots of extra pounds, with two babies in diapers, two babies drinking bottles, two babies crying, and a husband devoting his time and emotional energy to a new job. *Help!*

On the positive side of the ledger, I was also unprepared for falling completely and totally in love with these little people who have been entrusted to my care. I was unprepared for my heart skipping beats when I think about these little ones who are the dearest things that my heart has ever known. I was unprepared for being excited about waking them up in the morning because I missed them and was anxious to see what funny, cute things they would do that day. I was unprepared for the joy and pride I feel when they exhibit their kindness, love, intelligence, or developing faith.

Lori Solyom, who had done a variety of interesting, challenging jobs before having children, says this about her first daughter: "She didn't care what I had done or what I could do—she just wanted to be nursed, changed, and rocked constantly. *I was a mother with no mothering skills!* I was completely unprepared for this demanding little person—how much I would love her, how much she would need me—how inadequate and inept I would feel in trying to meet her needs."

It is important to remember when we are experiencing some of the less pleasant surprises of motherhood that there are so many unexpected delights as well. Some mothers keep a mother's journal, diligently recording everything their child does. Along with or instead of a traditional mother's journal, how about keeping a list of the unexpected, wonderful, cute, charming, deep, and adorable things your child does or says? Then, on a bad day, you can take out this memory book and be refreshed and reminded that motherhood is a job with many compensations.

God never sends us more than we can handle. And in handling and managing things, hopefully we grow to some sense of maturity and a place of peace.

Expectations of Full-Time Mothering

We have all seen the blissful commercial on television. The new mother is rocking her baby in the nursery. The room is perfectly furnished with white, wispy, fluffy curtains, blankets, and spreads. The mother is wearing a long, white nightgown and has beautiful hair and a beautifully made-up face. And all her laundry is freshly done in a pile beside her. To some extent, this is what we might expect life at home with children to be like. But reality may be much different, as authors Sanders and Bullen point out:

> Both first-time mothers and experienced mothers who have recently left the work force expect the most unreasonable things of themselves as at-home mothers. They assume that taking care of a baby will not be very difficult and will leave them with lots of free time to explore their own projects. They imagine that the house will be sparkling, they'll have cookies in the oven, and they'll still have time to read to their children and work on their dissertations.[7]

In reality, a good day for you may be when you are able to shower by noon. And that's okay. You have a new agenda, and there are no rules about what time of day your hair has to be washed.

For many of us who were accustomed to a very structured day, this lack of structure can be maddening. But it is an opportunity for you to make your own structure, based on your priorities for yourself and your family. There is a rhythm to our mothering that we alone set. Some women have a somewhat-scheduled day with classes, lessons, and story hours. Others find bliss in taking their time in the morning and not getting out of jammies until ten. What is important for you to do this day? Is it important to make a memory with your child or to clean the basement? There is time for both, but don't forget to do the most important things first.

What can you realistically get done at home, and what is truly important for you to do? The work never ends, and there are constant interruptions. There will always be laundry. You might not have time to write the great American novel or finish your dissertation while your baby is crying a lot. But don't forget that these moments are fleeting. Soon your children will need you less, and you can pursue other interests.

Remember that a mother's most important work has eternal significance—the raising and nurturing of a child of God.

Defining Your New Role

Authors Darcie Sanders and Martha Bullen advise us to know what we want our job to be at home. Do we want to focus our talents on being the teacher of our children, or a community activist, or the administrator of a home-based business?[8] Whatever your focus, your whole family needs to know what the definition of your role is.

My friend Marnie Murray told me a story about hearing her eighteen-month-old stuffing clothes into a drawer one day and chanting, "Mommy's not the maid. Mommy's not the maid." Marnie realized she had said that more than once to her children. But it is something they needed to have clarified. It is something husbands need to work out with wives as well.

Arlene Cardozo says, "For the woman who chooses to sequence to be expected—because she is 'home anyway'—to do all the housework would be to repeat the mistakes of the generation of the 1960s, when many of the mothers who fled from home threw out the baby with the bath water."[9] Being home does not mean being totally responsible for chores and errands. In fact, Cardozo notes that, "most of today's couples set all housework into a category completely separate from caring for the children." Another of Cardozo's factors that differentiate the woman who is happy at home from the woman who is not, is "the woman's making a very clear distinction between the children and the work of the house with a minimum of her time spent on the house and maximum on the family."[10]

One bad day I described myself as a minutia manager. It was a day of diarrhea, failed attempts at potty training, and other unpleasantries. A friend called and asked me what I was doing, and I realized that about 40 percent of what I had done that day required rubber gloves and disinfectant. But if I choose to focus on the number of spills I wipe up, or the daily diaper count, I will have missed the point of my being home—to raise, shape, enjoy, play with, influence, and grow with our children.

Even though my husband works many hours, we realize that housework is not just *my job*: If I make the clear distinction between the tasks of maintaining the house and the vocation of raising the children, I am much happier being home. When I lose this focus, I spend too much time mumbling and grumbling in the laundry room and feeling sorry for myself.

If your house is not a showplace, who cares! If your family is happy and well cared for, the rest is inconsequential.

Mourning the Loss of Your Working World Support System

I think I enjoyed some of the trappings of practicing law more than the actual practice. I liked being in a certain social circle. I liked having important friends. I liked feeling like a big shot.

When I first came home to raise our children, I had a hard time getting my ego through the door. I can remember going under the table three (or more) times a day to clean up the floor after meals. Under the table I would mutter to myself, "I shouldn't have to do this! I've got all this education! I should be trying jury trials in court!" Yet there I was, under the table, without my old social system to support me. I knew I had to pull out my bitterness, take a good look at it, and get rid of it.

When I ran into a sticky problem while practicing law, I had trusted colleagues who I could call any time for advice and counsel. When I was home with our children, with no mother of my own and my mother-in-law six hours away, I had to assemble a new support system. I had to meet some new people who were doing the really important job of raising their families. As a result of reaching out and being vulnerable, open, and willing to learn from others, I believe I have deeper, more spiritual friendships than I have ever had before.

As a mother, you don't get performance evaluations. There aren't prescribed standards for you to meet, so you don't know if you're doing a good job. It isn't black and white like a jury verdict. But your season at home can be a marvelous time to set your own standards for yourself and your children. One woman in Arlene Cardozo's book established a goal she felt was appropriate:

> . . . that my children should see in each day something special, that we do some special things together—it doesn't take much to please a child, you know—picking apples from a neighbor's tree, making cookies, making up dance steps to a new record, going skating, a trip to the library. In a way, doing special things seems to be a really short-term goal. But if each day has something special, and it's a happy experience, all the days should add up to a pretty special childhood for each of them . . . and that's essentially what I want them to have and what I want to help provide.[11]

Think about how long it took you to learn and feel comfortable at your last job. You not only had to acquire the skills and the knowledge to do the job, but you also had to get to know the people you were working with. Finally, you had to figure out how to pace your work and take care of yourself so you could perform effectively.

You will go through the same on-the-job adjustment period as a mother at home. You'll have to find your own solutions to learning the skills, meeting the people, and pacing yourself. Cut yourself some slack. Like any important endeavor, it takes time.

Find a Good Baby-Sitter—For Your Own Sake

The isolation of being a new mother at home can be devastating. We'll talk about support groups and other resources later on in the book. But next to having the unequivocal support of your husband, you can be your own best supporter. I have realized that part of giving support to myself is taking a break now and then. I don't have anyone patting me on the back and telling me what a great job I did scrubbing that toilet, so I have to find other compensations. Mine is solitude.

When finding a new support system, one of my greatest discoveries was baby-sitters. When I first came home, I was so hungry for the company of our children that I sneered at the idea of hiring a sitter so I could have some time alone. I was also maniacal about family time and insisted that we go everywhere together. What a difference a year makes! I have discovered that a few hours here and there with a caregiver will not harm our children, especially when they have spent 99.9 percent of their time with me. They actually enjoy the break in their routine and the time spent with a different person. And I am relearning how to relish solitude—like shopping without a toddler hanging on me or my shopping cart or driving in absolute silence without Mother Goose blaring on the tape player.

There is so much joy to life with children. But part of supporting yourself to do the best job you can is accepting the joy of a few stolen hours away from them, too.

Depression

It is not easy to admit suffering from postpartum depression. In fact, it took me months to tell anyone other than my husband.

We really wanted our second baby. She came a mere seventeen months after her sister. My husband was contemplating a job change that would have far-reaching career and logistical implications for me. We had money concerns like every other young couple we knew. But all these difficulties were nothing compared to the devastation I felt after bringing home our daughter.

The first week or so went well. My in-laws were there to help, and my husband took time off work. I was exhausted, sore, and worried, but I was still wrapped in that warm blanket of excitement over a new baby. The challenges seemed inconsequential compared to the joy I felt holding our daughter.

But the baby didn't sleep, the toddler got disoriented and jealous, the in-laws went home, and my husband went back to work. Exhausted and now overwhelmed, I sank into a depression a few weeks after giving birth. Even though I was tired, I couldn't sleep. My mind whirred and hummed with my worries and concerns, keeping me wide awake while the children napped and waking me during the night. Where was the joy and euphoria of new motherhood? Instead I felt inadequate and very, very afraid of the depression that enveloped me.

But fortunately my episode of postpartum depression was short-lived and relatively mild. I got some good medical advice and had a very supportive husband. With some vitamin and mineral supplements and extra rest, I was soon managing my new responsibilities and enjoying my life again.

If you suffer from postpartum depression, you may feel ashamed and want to hide it. You may feel it is somehow your fault. Such a reaction, however, can make the time even more difficult to endure. Consider the massive changes your body went through during your pregnancy and childbirth. Given the enormous disruption of hormones and brain chemicals, a postpartum depression, which has both physical and psychological components, is understandable. If you are suffering from such a reaction, you need to address it in your mind, body, and spirit.

Don't hesitate to ask for help. The sooner you ask, the sooner you will feel better. Most gynecologists are sensitive to the needs of a postpartum woman. If yours is not, get another opinion. Treatment for postpartum depression can range from simple nutrient supplementation to progesterone therapy to the use of anti-depressant medication in the most severe cases.

An excellent book on the subject is *The New Mother Syndrome: Coping With Postpartum Stress and Depression* by Carol Dix (New York: Pocket Books, 1985). A newsletter and other supportive information is available from a group called D.A.D., which stands for Depression After Delivery. They can be contacted at P.O. Box 1282, Morrisville, PA 19067, (215) 295-3994.

Also, be patient with yourself and your new child, and remember the wisdom of Philippians 4:6–7: "Do not be anxious about anything, but in everything, by prayer and petition, with thanksgiving, present your requests to God. And the peace of God, which transcends all understanding, will guard your hearts and minds in Christ Jesus."

Although I felt like my postpartum depression would never end, one day the clouds lifted, and the joy of mothering began again. You will live through this time, and it will ultimately strengthen you and your bond to your child.

Guilt

Some days when my husband comes home I am seriously unraveled. One of the great mysteries of parenting is that these little people can be so lovable yet sometimes so irritating.

One day in particular stands out. We were in the throes of deciding whether or not to move, Caitlin had colic, Clare was needy because this new little person was taking up all of mom's time, and I was in my postpartum depression. About five minutes before my husband was due home I left both kids crying in their cribs and went to the porch to have a good cry myself. When my husband pulled up, he had to talk me into going back inside and dealing with my responsibilities.

I have since learned to earnestly pray in times like this. Instead of feeling guilty for being so unraveled, I now turn to the only Source that can ever knit me back together again. Sometimes I let the children hear me praying for patience. It is an oddity of our nature that we can feel so guilty about one of the things that can restore us and help us to be better moms—time for ourselves, and more importantly, time for our relationship with God. Marilee Horton talks about the importance of time with God:

> This, sad to say, is the easiest relationship to neglect, because He doesn't put up a fuss. He just patiently waits until we miss Him so much we get back into fellowship. . . . If it seems that you are being pulled apart by your responsibilities, you would do yourself a favor by making time for your Heavenly Father. He really loves you and He just wants a few minutes of your undivided attention. If you will ask Him, I believe He will make a time and a way for you, so your day will run smoother and your nerves will be less frayed.[12]

Don't feel guilty about needing time for yourself or for your devotions. It will ultimately help you stay whole and connected to God, and your whole family will benefit.

Money Matters

I was terrified to lose my income. I have been earning my own money and been financially self-sufficient since I was in my teens. I was afraid of being dependent on my husband.

From the beginning of our marriage, I managed the money. I paid the bills, handled the checkbook and investments, and ran up the credit cards. I didn't do a great job of money management, yet I didn't trust my husband to do it either. My need to be in control of these things was a symptom of my lack of trust in my husband, and ultimately, my lack of trust in God's plan for our lives.

Money can often be a battleground for couples because it is a powerful thing. In fact, some people define their power by money. "The fears that some women have about losing their incomes are based on the belief that economics determines the power distribution in the marriage,"[13] Arlene Cardozo points out.

I heard a story about a lawyer who kept her husband in line by telling him that all she had to do was to press "PRINT." What she meant was that for her, getting divorced would be as easy as pressing a command on her computer that would print out her divorce papers. She could then file them, go to court and represent herself, and be divorced—no muss, no fuss. At the time I thought this was a somewhat amusing story. I am now struck by sadness that she viewed marriage as so disposable. To her way of thinking, she was self-supporting—why did she *need* a husband who was giving her grief?

The need to control and manage money may be based on the belief that money does equal power. Part of it may also be a lack of faith and commitment to your marriage. Your husband may earn the money at this time, but it is money for the family. As a couple, you need to nourish the idea that the contribution you each make to the marriage is vital. When you feel secure in that, the issue of who manages the money is not so emotionally loaded.

Remember that someday you will in all likelihood earn money again. There will be another season of monetary productiveness. But for now, your financial contribution can be learning to save and use money wisely.

Fulfillment Is Where You Find It

What is fulfillment anyway? "I would describe fulfillment as being in the place God wants me to be and enjoying it. Contentment equals fulfillment," says author Marilee Horton.[14]

---

*W**hat do you enjoy least about being home?***

Being interrupted by the kids when I have a big task. It also gets monotonous sometimes.
                                                    —*Jewel Wolfe*

If our happiness depends on our circumstances, we are in trouble. Our circumstances may change hourly, but our fulfillment as Christian women comes from Christ. Paul said it best: "I have learned the secret of being content in any and every situation, whether well fed or hungry, whether living in plenty or in want. I can do everything through him who gives me strength" (Phil. 4:12b–13).

What is the source of power in your life? Is it a career and money or material things? These power sources won't bring you contentment or fulfillment, no matter how much you've been led to believe they will. Plugging into God's power source leads to real peace and fulfillment. Put God in control of your life, give your marriage and your children over to him, and he will give you fulfillment.

You have heard the popular expression, "Bloom where you are planted." The true way to bloom is to discover the gifts God has given you and use them to serve him. The Bible tells us, "Each one should use whatever gift he has received to serve others, faithfully administering God's grace in its various forms" (1 Peter 4:10). If you have searched your heart and asked God to send you children, your gift is to be their mother. It is a unique job which no one else can perform. Accept the role joyfully and fulfillment will follow.

5

What Happened to My Self-Esteem?

Prior to taking the job, my image of motherhood was not positive. As a result, some of my mothering experiences have not been positive, and I have struggled with my self-esteem since coming home to raise our children.

My mother was severely depressed, stressed, and worn out after raising eight children. Watching her as an adolescent, I became determined to be a different kind of mother. For the most part, my home has a different feel from the home of my childhood. There is more laughter. There is more joy. Yet while making the transition to my current comfort-zone of mothering, my self-esteem took a beating. It has survived, strengthened in faith, but reaching this point has been far from easy.

Why is it important for a mother to maintain good self-esteem? Because the way we feel about ourselves is transmitted to our children. We are their mirrors. Dr. Evelyn Silten Bassoff explains, "When children sense that their mother suffers from low self-esteem, they may suppress their own needs for recognition and approval and devote themselves to bolstering her self-image and to meeting her needs: They may become her sparkling mirror."[1]

I can remember spending much of my energy in childhood trying to make my mother happy, to make her smile, or, on a really good day, to make her laugh. That was not my job. My job was to play and work on growing up, not be my mother's cheerleader. Our children have more important, healthier work to do than bolstering their mother's sagging self-esteem.

We need to take care of ourselves so that we can take care of our children. We need to make sure our needs are being met by our faith, husbands, relatives, and friends so that we don't turn to our children to mirror back our worth. If we feel good about our work as mothers and realize its value and significance, we will feel good about ourselves, and our children will have healthy, positive self-esteem modeled for them. Our children watch us to learn how to take care of themselves. We need to be good models for them, meeting the needs of our families while also tending to our own.

It is obvious that we want our children to have good self-esteem, but how important is it to them? Idene Goldman, teacher and consultant, says that, "Children with high self-esteem, that is those who respect themselves and have a feeling of self worth, are happier, have fewer illnesses, are more accepted by others, have more friends, and do better in school than children with low self-esteem."[2] Every mother wants that for her child.

Why do mothers struggle with self-esteem? Part of the problem is that our culture does not truly value our work. Raising the next generation is not seen as important. "The feminist trivialization of motherhood not only did damage to the self-esteem of large numbers of women, it presented to women a new definition of womanhood that stands at odds with the reality of most women's lives and feelings."[3] Many of our mothers were brought up with a life goal of raising a family, and that was a good goal. However, succeeding generations were told by our culture that your value as a woman is measured by how high you climb in a corporation or how much money you make. Marnie Murray says, "Our society does not value nurturing and care taking. It values achievement, especially financial success. Stay-at-home parents are second-class citizens."

Those of us whose hearts lean towards home may feel inferior to the superwoman who is conquering the world, and as a result we may suffer from low self-esteem. But guess what? Many of the women who have bought into the male definition of success are wondering about their choice. Many of our sisters are looking at us, and wondering if their path is worthwhile.

> *What do you enjoy most about being home?*
>
> **The unexpected, deep questions they ask.**
> —*Jewel Wolfe*

Those of us who have left careers to come home may also suffer a lessened sense of self-esteem because our new roles require such different skills. Lori Solyom says her diminished self-esteem was "mostly a reflection on the great deal of confidence I had always felt on the job and the complete lack of it I had in my new role as mommy."

Either way, the self-doubt that women feel about their chosen life goals or lifestyle can lead to feelings of low self-esteem. I believe that some soul-searching, clarification of goals, and, most importantly, strengthening our relationship with Christ (by realizing the attributes of our identity in Christ) are the remedies for low self-esteem.

Psychologist Dr. Joyce Block dealt with issues of mothers' self-esteem and changes in identity in the book *Motherhood as*

Metamorphosis: Change and Continuity in the Life of a New Mother.
She goes into great depth on the enormous emotional changes
that many of us experience when we become mothers. She
says:

> If a new mother is filled with doubt about her choices or
> even questions her ability to choose correctly, she will, in
> all likelihood, be more easily swayed by the opinions of oth-
> ers. If, moreover, this doubt is associated with generally low
> self-esteem, a woman may find herself vacillating at every
> juncture and every time she encounters someone who has
> a different opinion. Insecurity feeds upon itself, and the
> more such a mother looks outside herself for "solutions" to
> her problems, the more she flounders and the less she trusts
> her own judgment.[4]

I believe we need to stop looking outside ourselves for
answers to the trials of motherhood, and start looking inside ourselves and to our God. As we become more rooted
in our faith and in our relationship with God, we become
better mothers. Remember, "Every good and perfect gift is
from above, coming down from the Father of the heavenly
lights, who does not change like shifting shadows" (James
1:17). Our feelings about motherhood may change, but if
our trust in God is strong and our commitment to mothering is unwavering, we will not be shifting shadows in our
homes and families. Jodi Benware says, "I know I have the
most important career of all—that of raising godly children
with Christian values."

Another factor affecting a mother's self-esteem is simply
day-to-day life with children. It is far from glamorous. When
noon rolls around and you are still in your bathrobe with
spit-up on your shoulder, you may not be feeling the best
about yourself. You may wonder if you will ever be able to
function effectively out in the "real world" again. Debbi
Heinze jokes that, "No one ever said, 'You did a great job

with that diaper rash!'" But for mothers at home, the reality of day-to-day life with small children *is* the real world. Instead of comparing ourselves to everyone else and scrutinizing our lives under the microscope of what our culture values, how about just valuing the life that we have and cherishing this time with our children?

Susan Fenton says her self-esteem has been enhanced since she became a full-time mom. "Despite some days of struggling with low self-esteem, feeling I'm not really working, my overall sense of self worth has increased. I feel content with the simple things of our daily life. . . . I am blessed to be involved with the true realities of life. . . . It is life in a simple, basic form, and I savor it. . . . I feel this life *is* my reality . . . that much of the rest of our fast paced, urgent society is less real. Watching my kids 'just be' has freed me to be more real—more alive."

Barbara Trudel, another mom at home, considers her life "a work in progress. In that sense, I look upon these years at home with our children as one facet of my life and an important step in my overall career. And while I admire the do-it-all moms who can juggle tiny tots, life at home, a marriage, and a career, I know that I'm just not one of those women. I sometimes wonder if those women exist or if they're just very good at pretending that they can do it all and do it well."

Many women report that coming home has been a time of self-discovery. Sue Ekins says, "In some ways, I've found myself." Nancy V. notes, "When I finally became a mother, I felt my self-esteem rise, and I felt like I had become more of a whole person." Mary Hotwagner says, "The things I've learned at home about myself will carry through in the future. I'm much more confident."

A mother's self-esteem can be bolstered by the realization that hers is a job with eternal significance. We are raising our children to love the Lord and to help spread that love to the world. Jana Trovato says, "I know it is a significant job in God's eyes." Cheryl Ammons holds the same belief, a belief that she arrived at after some struggle. She says, "After I dealt with feelings of being left out and wrestled with God about my role as mother and my responsibility to him, my husband, and my children, my self-esteem has been increased because I have the most important job in the world. I must find my worth in the Lord."

Norma Kunda points out, "People get too hung up on the idea of self-esteem. First of all," she says, "my worth is rooted in Jesus Christ and the sacrifice he made for me. God thought I was valuable enough to give his only Son's life for me. Also, I know I'm doing the job God wants me to do and is enabling me to do. Right now, this is the best job on earth for me—and the one that only I can do. Therefore, my self-esteem in enhanced. The only times it is diminished is when I succumb to the attacks of those who tell me I'm wasting my education and such, and when my thinking gets off the right track. Fortunately, those times are usually quite brief, because I really do know that my current job is the very best use of all my abilities."

Listening to the world or the media can be detrimental. Brenda Passon says, "When I listen to the world, my self-esteem could be diminished, but when I think about what is best for my family, I know I'm doing the right thing."

As a mother at home, you can take pride in the work you are doing. Kerry Mattson says, "I think my self-esteem is improved now because I am proud that I have put my family first." Marnie Murray says, "It is my vocation." Karen Gresk says her self-esteem is enhanced "when people say my children are doing wonderfully." Denise Wickline says her self-esteem is enhanced by staying home, "Because I'm doing something that has eternal value and great significance." The confidence you gain from that knowledge is worth more than any self-esteem booster the world can provide.

A Series of Seasons

It is becoming an increasingly popular notion to view your life as a series of seasons, but the Bible talked about it first: "There is a time for everything, and a season for every activity under heaven" (Eccles. 3:1). The time of raising children is one short season. Many preceded it and many will follow. Perhaps the shortness of the season is what makes it so sweet.

Dr. Hunter says, "We are only home for a season. Since our time at home is short, let us make the most of the summer. Then with positive memories we embrace more fully the world beyond our doorstep. We can dance into a winter of rich reward, rather than shuffle into a season of regret."[5]

What do you enjoy least about being home?

The difficulty in getting around with both children.

—Cheryl Ammons

Nature recognizes the pattern of seasons as well. We don't ignore or fight the coming of winter because there is nothing we can do about it. Yet sometimes we women ignore the rhythm of the seasons of our lives to pursue our own agendas. Author Debbie Barr says this is because, as humans, we can make choices and can choose to override what is natural for a given season of life. "But in God's economy," she says, "there is a time designated for accomplishing everything he has called us to do and gifted us to pursue."[6]

Just as our lives follow a pattern of seasons, so do the lives of our children. As they come into a season of maturing, a

season of more personal freedom arrives for their mother.
If we can synchronize the seasons, both mothers and children can reap the benefit of focused attention and care. With
our focus clear and our priorities in order, we can move easily from one season to another with no regrets.

6

You'll Always Be a Mother, but Your Kids Only Have One Childhood

There's an old Irish expression that says, "When God made time, he made plenty of it." These days, you wonder. I saw a man running an errand to the dry cleaner. His three children were in the back seat—two in car seats. They were eating macaroni and cheese off of paper plates. I thought of our daughters laughing and fighting around the dinner table and praying their grace prayer. We have the luxury of time, on most nights, to savor our food (as much as one can savor anything with small children) and to share our lives. "Tell us something good that happened today," we sometimes ask our children. On a good night, we laugh and talk and enjoy our time together.

Time—The Greatest Gift I Can Give My Children

A nearby suburb proudly announced the opening of a child care center near the commuter train. With a dry cleaner

next door and a cash machine nearby, parents can drop off
their kids and their laundry, hit the cash machine, and jump
on the train all in one stop. Why does this depress me so?
Do we value our time as much as we value our children?
"Don't waste my precious time," we tell those who distract
us. Are our children trying to tell us, "Don't waste our precious childhood"?

I compulsively planned my schedule my last year of practicing law in order to maximize my time at home. I had rules:
No appointments after 3 P.M.; no court on Friday. But I still
felt driven, fragmented, and unable to relax and enjoy either
role. And so I came home. For a while, our days at home
were sheer impulse. We would dash off for this or that and
come back feeling tired and unfulfilled. The mind-set, although not the dollar value, of my scheduled time as a lawyer
carried over. A good day was measured by how much I got
done. I can remember proudly ticking off my accomplish-
ments to my husband at the end of the day: I painted one
wall, and I cleaned out three drawers. Aren't I wonderful?

There was an urgency to my mothering. The kids and I
simply had to have certain experiences or do certain activities, or I wouldn't be doing the mother-thing right. I pushed
our schedules and over-filled our days when all my children
really wanted was my time. Some days we were in and out
of the car so much that I was tired from the sheer effort of
lifting and moving them to and from their car seats. Was all
this really necessary? Could I plan my life to avoid excess
errands? I realized I needed to reevaluate when our kids
began mentioning shopping as one of their favorite activities. I like to shop, but there are certainly other things to do
for fun. I am seeking a balance between compulsively planning my days and impulsively squandering my time.

It is true that when God made time, he made plenty of
it. We just need the wisdom to know how to use it wisely.
I used to define "wise use of my time" by the dollar value
attached to my services as an attorney. "Is it worth my time

to do this?" was the measuring stick I used to evaluate my commitments.

It took a long, long time for me to set aside my ego, my drivenness, and my need for recognition and self-importance to realize that wiping noses, feeding, cleaning, cuddling, and meeting our children's needs was the best use of my time. It also took me a long time to accept that not all time with children is blissful. But we need to live fully all of the times, both the good and the not so good.

> *What do you enjoy most about being home?*
>
> *The flexibility of my schedule and freedom to do things I enjoy, such as gardening and cooking, that I was unable (and usually too tired) to do when I was working full-time away from my home.*
>
> *—Nancy V.*

The Value of Not-So-Blissful Times

I was sick. I was lying-under-the-electric-blanket-set-on-ten-and-shivering sick. My husband couldn't get away from work, my aunt was busy, and my sister was at school.

At first, the girls played nicely. Then they fought. Then they played. Then they fought. I missed the luxury of being able to lie in bed, watch talk shows, and moan. Our girls needed me. I couldn't ignore them, as much as I tried. Young children insinuate themselves into your sickroom and force you to pay attention to them.

My brain raced with options. Did I have enough energy to pack up the car and take them to a paid sitter? No. The mere thought made me tired. Did a neighbor or someone in my baby-sitting co-op owe me some time? Yes, but it would still take too much energy to arrange.

I am constantly learning that sometimes the best way out is through. On those days when the kids are beasties, and I want to get away from them, I hold them. I sit down and play with them, and they become nicer children. Could slowing down and savoring my sick day moment by moment make it more bearable?

That day, we learned how to fold towels together. We used plastic knives to cut fresh green beans and cheese. We stuck pretzel sticks in the cheese for snacks. We did Play-Doh and markers. We took our time with each activity and turned a dreadful day into a slow, savored time together. We somehow grew closer by sharing a difficult time. Once again, simple pleasures are the best way to delight in the day the Lord has made, no matter what it brings.

> *What do you enjoy least about being home?*
>
> *Long days alone with three preschoolers!*
>   *—Jana Trovato*

Being Here

God was not done stretching me yet. When I got over the shock of my radical change of lifestyle, I began to realize that while I was present physically—changing the diapers, wiping the wall—my mind was a million miles away.

God changed my heart on one of the worst days of being home with small children. You know the days—the kids are driving you crazy, you feel you have no purpose, and you hate the life you have. God put the thought into my head,

"Well, this is it, Chris. This is your life. You can learn to relax, enjoy, and love it, or you will squander it."

I used to look back on the preparatory times of my life as the most memorable. Preparing for a career, preparing for marriage, trying to have children—these were all exciting, growth-filled times. But now those times are done. While there are certainly exciting challenges ahead, for right now—this is my life. My days are filled with the thousand mundane tasks of daily life with small children. On a really bad day, all I could see were the piles of dirty clothes and all the other work to be done. But if this was *it*, I had to learn to make the best of it, or I would have missed my life—not to mention the lives of our children. If this was *it*, I had to learn to concentrate on the squeals and laughter, the hugs and kisses, the love and the fun. The years are already adding up.

On a really bad day, I put the answering machine on and order out for dinner. Then I sit on the floor and let our beautiful children show me their world—how they like to play, what they think about, and what's important to them. One slow, summer day, Clare lifted her lovely face to mine and said, "Mommy, it's a beautiful world."

When I stop comparing my present life to what it once was, when I can stop obsessing about what it will be in the future, I can truly say it is wonderful just to be here. I can only pray that our children will remember having my relatively undivided attention during their early years with joy. They'll be gone before I know it.

What Is a Home?

Because the home of my childhood fell short in many ways, I had to come to my own definition of home. I believe that home should be a place where people build one another up, accept one another's faults, and give and receive love unconditionally.

Home should be a place where people freely give their love and help to one another, without grumbling or complaining, but out of love and compassion.

Home should be a peaceful place of rest where we can go to be refreshed. Home should be a place of fun and creativity where we can express ourselves and share in the joy of life together.

Home should be a place of open communication where good communication skills are learned. I don't mean there should be no fighting, but that disagreements should be handled with respect and dignity and that we should take the time to really listen to one another.

Home should be a place of celebration. Celebrating the family and the home is a way to show gratitude for your blessings. Celebrating is a way to distinguish the specialness of each day. You can celebrate anything with your children: the first day of spring, the first snowfall, the last day of school, learning to tie a shoe.

There are also small traditions that make a house a home—having a special tea together, taking a bubble bath, or watching certain TV shows as a family. These small things are traditions that shape your family life. They are everyday ways to celebrate life and to rejoice in the days the Lord has given us.

What about Older Children?

How many children do you know who come home to empty houses after school? Too many. The world of school is no picnic. Children can be cruel and thoughtless to one another. A day at school can be a serious challenge to values and self-esteem. What effect does it have on the child to come home to an empty house? "If we aren't there when our school-aged children return home, we may never hear about the pressures or triumphs of the day. Many mothers find that by the time they arrive home at five or six o'clock from work, aerobics, or volunteer activities, their children's hearts are closed to them," says Dr. Brenda Hunter.[1]

Our society expects much more, much sooner from children today. They are expected to be able to manage the difficult separation of day care when they are very young. Then they are expected to waltz off to school without a care in the world. Then, when they are minimally self-sufficient, they are expected to be able to take care of themselves after school until their parents arrive at the doorstep, exhausted from their day and full of their own cares. Can we really expect a child to feel secure and to flourish emotionally under these circumstances?

Researcher Armand Nicholi studied drug users and discovered they have several things in common including spending a lot of time away from home, emotional distance from their parents, and relying on peers for emotional support. He believes that children use drugs to meet intense emotional needs. Where do these needs come from? "Nicholi blames parental absence, due to divorce, death, or a time-demanding job. Parental absence contributes to 'the anger, the rebelliousness, low self-esteem, depression and anti-social behavior' of the drug user."[2]

Some mothers say that young children are time consuming but that the pre-adolescent or adolescent is the child who really needs your time and encouragement. With the pressures facing young people now including school, gangs, and drugs, we need to protect them and look out for them even more.

Psychologist and author Dr. Anthony Moriarty assessed the risks of an adolescent becoming involved in a gang. He laments that many young people (the so-called latch-key kids) are growing up on their own. Many suffer from parental neglect because their parents are too preoccupied, and school and peer pressures are greater than ever. All of these factors increase the risk that a child will be attracted to gang membership. Parental involvement to keep kids out of gangs is critical. "Parents are the key to successful prevention and early intervention," Dr. Moriarty states.[3]

Our children's need for us does not end when they walk out the door to school. In many ways, they need us more as they mature. It is a difficult, confusing world out there. If we begin the good work of raising our children, we need to be committed to see it through to completion.

7

ᕯhe Mommy Wars

What are the mommy wars? They are often highly-emotional verbal battles between working mothers and stay-at-home mothers. A working mother participates any time she intentionally or thoughtlessly tries to make a stay-at-home mother feel inferior. And a stay-at-home mother participates whenever she tries to make a working mother feel guilty.

Sue Ekins, mother at home, says this of her experience: "'Working' moms have said things like, 'Your son talks pretty good, considering he's not in day care,' or 'I go crazy on the days I am home with my kids (like vacations). I'm all kidded-out and can't wait to get back to work. Being with kids all day drives me nuts.' The implication is that only a mindless, unmotivated person would want to be home; the workplace is where the challenges are." Jackie Wellwood, a home schooling mother of five says, "I find little affirmation for my decision to be at home. Having a large home schooling family further attracts stares and comments that make me feel as though I am swimming upstream."

You can have no doubt about my belief that it is better for children to have their mother home full-time. But if circumstances prevent a mother from making a full-time commitment to mothering, it is not our responsibility or place to judge her. Before having a family, I had some attitudes and preconceived notions that I had to reevaluate when I became a stay-at-home mom. I can actually remember asking a mother, "What do you do all day?" with intended superiority in my voice. Now that I know the answer to that question, I have wished for forgiveness for my ignorance and intolerance.

"Asking a woman I've just met at a cocktail party how she spends her day is something I may never try again. Women who 'don't work'—that is, who work at home as mothers—sometimes visibly bridle. Mothers who work full-time outside the home often feel compelled to mention how worthwhile their work is or how wonderful their day care center is. The feelings about both lifestyles have heated up tremendously in the last several years," says author Christine Davidson.[1]

Feelings were particularly strong in the early stages of the feminist movement. Mothers at home were seen as slothful, lazy, and lacking ambition. Oddly enough, with the swing back to raising children at home, many stay-at-home moms now view their working sisters as cold, selfish, overly ambitious, and uncaring. A mother in either situation will have no trouble finding someone who disagrees with her choice. What we need to do is to tune out the clatter of the world that tells us how to live our lives and look instead to our own hearts. Is there love enough in your heart to accept the choice or the circumstance of a sister who must work? Whether working out of the home or at home, young or old, we can learn from one another. The mommy wars accomplish nothing and diminish all of us.

The women's movement has helped us make strides in our roles in society, yet has resulted in a devaluing of our roles at home. While choices for women have been expanded, the choice of the mother at home has not been a valued one. Pamela Piljac explains, "Rather than support women at home by providing alternatives for their problems, the new movement told them that they required freedom *from* their home and family to maintain a job outside the home. This was the prescription for fulfillment and prestige."[2]

Referring to the work of Gloria Steinem, Betty Friedan, and Germaine Greer, author Dr. Brenda Hunter expresses her anger at the shortsightedness of feminists:

> I am angry that these women used their impressive intellects to shape social policy without first examining and understanding their own personal histories. A whole generation of women has marched to their misguided anti-marriage, anti-male, and anti-family music. . . . In the end, we women have to look to our own families and ask what our children need. As we shall see, youth in this country have not flourished during the more than two decades of contemporary feminism.[3]

A new view of women in our society would embrace and support the choices of all women—whether working outside or inside the home. It would recognize and accommodate the different seasons of a woman's life and would allow her to pursue her dreams one at a time.

Why should we resent the woman who toils all day at the workplace then comes home to all the undone tasks that we may have had time to take care of during the day? Can you honestly say you envy the fatigue and stress she must experience? And why should the working woman resent our quiet life at home when she might be able to try it on for size and see if it suits her? There are certain experiences that are universal to all mothers. "The truth is that at-home and working mothers have a lot in common. They are all dealing with the same challenges of parenting—sleepless nights, toilet training, battles with two-year-olds and adolescents, and raising their children the best way they can—but have come up with different solutions," conclude authors Darcie Sanders and Martha Bullen.[4]

I believe that we do not change society by legislative pronouncements and legal maneuvering. The world will change through the constructive celebration and encouragement of one-on-one relationships. Authors Sanders and Bullen say, "The best solution to this mutual resentment is to work at creating authentic relationships between at-home and working mothers. If you want participation from employed mothers, make an effort to keep community events accessible. Consider scheduling some of these events on weekends or in the evening. . . . Don't affirm yourself by putting someone else down. . . . The other mothers are your sisters."[5]

But you don't need to wait for a sanctioned community event to express your willingness to be a source of help and encouragement to your working neighbors. How about giving them a few hours of baby-sitting so they can go to the grocery store alone once in a while? Or offering to take their child along with you on a Saturday morning outing so she can have some catch-up time at home?

I hope that the term "mommy wars" will one day be obsolete. We all love our children, and we need to focus on our love instead of our differences.

> *What do you enjoy most about being home?*
>
> **Knowing my children feel loved and respected and important.**
> —Linda Jenkins

Mothers in Society

In the last few political campaigns, we heard lip service paid to family values and the worth of mothers. Some people were heartened by this. Others saw it as political windbagging.

Try spending a day out in the world with a child (or children) to experience the reality of society's concern for mothers and children. Some of the hazards you will encounter are candy-laden check-out counters in stores, restrooms without changing tables (even in establishments that cater to children), restaurants without high chairs, doors and aisles too narrow for strollers, and many other neglectful accommodations.

> Every mother can recount some shocking story of blatant mistreatment by someone in a public place who was offended by the very sight of her children. But as unsettling as such experiences are, they are not the main source of frustration many mothers feel as they try to function in American society. Rather, when a woman becomes a mother, she begins to experience a subtle kind of neglect, an unintentional thoughtlessness that manifests itself in hundreds of small ways, as she goes about her routine, daily business.[6]

It's the small things, magnified over hundreds of errands and forays into the marketplace with our children during the period we are home with them that lead some of us to conclude that we are not welcomed or valued.

Progress is being made, however. Some businesses provide play areas for children. Many public restrooms now have changing tables. These are small steps, but they are ways the marketplace can acknowledge the needs of mothers. And it makes good business sense. After all, who are the consumers? Who shops to buy the goods and services? It is the mothers, the organizers and procurers for their homes.

The Changing Workplace of America

Many working women want to come home. Many women at home would love to contribute to the family finances if they could do it in a way that would not compromise their commitment to their family. If our society values mothers and the work we do at home, it needs to take a look at the kind of support government and business could provide. The authors of *What's a Smart Woman Like You Doing at Home?* offer several suggestions.[7]

- Tax relief could be provided for families with children, perhaps a reduction for families in general or an increase in personal exemptions.
- Employers could provide more family-friendly employment by increasing part-time positions, job-sharing, and flex-time.
- Home-based employment opportunities could be explored by more businesses. With a computer and a telephone, many jobs can be performed at home.

These authors foresee a revolution in American motherhood with a new American mother emerging—one who puts family first, yet does not put herself last, and who is willing to find a creative balance between personal, economic, and family needs. We can help our daughters inherit this legacy by striving to model that balance in our own lives.

Handling Peer and Media Pressure

Did you know that stay-at-home moms are fashionable again, even a status symbol?! Does this picture sound like you? A recent front-page article in the *Wall Street Journal* depicting the new mother at home proclaimed, "This stay-at-home mom doesn't care about ring around the collar. She is the Power Mom, approaching motherhood as she once approached a profession. She is organizing $50,000 community fund raisers while holding down the equivalent of a part-time job in her child's classroom. She often hires full-time help because she is so busy."[8]

How absurd. I don't know who they're describing, but it sure ain't me! The other side of the spectrum is something like this: You're at a dinner, perhaps for your husband's work. The topic of what you do with your days inevitably arises. "I'm home with my kids," I have learned to reply. The inquirer's eyes glaze over, and he/she politely says, "How nice," while frantically scanning the room for someone more interesting to talk to. A few years ago, I was riveting. I could hold an entire dinner table of people captive with stories about the murder and sex abuse cases I had handled. Now, I am boring.

> *What do you enjoy least about being home?*
>
> **Tedium, repetitive chores, food preparation, cleaning up, and disciplining.**
> **—Cynthia McCabe**

For most of us, the truth lies somewhere between these extremes. We take pride in our mothering, but we don't look back or too far ahead so that we are always available to enjoy the present with our children. Linda Rush of the National Board of Directors of F. E.M.A.L.E. responded to the *Wall Street Journal* article by noting that a mom's motivations run deeper. "We make this choice to modify our paid work schedule for the benefit of our children, not our egos. The choice to spend more time with our children has gained a new respect over the years but it has not been and should not be at the expense of employed mothers. All mothers share a tremendous responsibility and society should not impose guilt on anyone for their work/family decisions."[9]

We, as mothers at home, can help women live with either choice by respecting one another's decisions. A choice should not be value laden. One choice is as valid as another. But mothers at home need to be encouraged to enjoy and relish their choice, rather than being left to wonder if they are supposed to be doing something else with their lives. And part of valuing our choice to be at home is refusing to feel put down because our lives are not more like those of our sisters in the marketplace.

In another interview Linda Rush noted that, "The more we can update the image of home-based mothers and make it realistic . . . the more comfortable people will be in their role as the primary caregiver of their children."[10] Cheryl Ammons, a mom at home, notes that, "I could care less what the media thinks. They are the ones missing out on God's best." Another mom, Jewel Wolfe, says, "I don't respect the media much, and I almost enjoy going against it." Janice Smullen, puts it this way: "I enjoy being out of the mainstream and love to set a precedent for others for such a worthwhile end result." It is this kind of confidence in our choice that will make our path easier and more appealing for the next generation. It is odd, though, that traditional choices are now being thought of as almost radical. Barbara Dafoe Whitehead, vice president of the Institute for Family Values, calls this a "growing familism; we're beginning to rethink where our main values lie."[11]

There is a new confidence among mothers-at-home. This confidence is born from doing what you believe is right, rather than trying to follow some culturally mandated agenda for your life. Mary Hotwagner puts it this way: "I feel we put the pressure on ourselves—if we are secure and happy with our choice, it shows and people don't force their opinions on us."

Barbara Trudel says, "In terms of what the mainstream of society thinks of at-home moms, I'd like to think that in this, the cusp of the 21st century, women (and men for that matter) should have every conceivable option open to them with regard to coping with the demands of career and family." This isn't always the case, though. Those of us who have chosen to stay at home face another challenge. Debbi Heinze says, "I'm afraid of that first interview with the career-woman-mom when I plan to return to work: How do I explain my being home without putting down her life?" Good question. An even better question is this: Why should we have to explain or justify our choice to stay home? If there is a gap in our résumé it is because we have been doing the crucial, passionate work of raising our children. Why should that be held against us?

8

Getting Support from Your Husband

One of the most delightful things my husband has ever done for me was my last birthday present. Our Sunday school teacher had just completed a class on family communication. We talked about active listening, reflective statements, and the enormous differences between the communication styles of men and women. (Women communicate on a feeling level. Men like to convey information and solve problems.) The class also touched on the idea of developing a family mission statement based on the work of Steven R. Covey and his book, *Principle-Centered Leadership*. To my delight, my husband presented me with a handsome, engraved plaque of "The Field Family Mission Statement" as my birthday present.

As a starting point for making a family mission statement, Covey suggests that you ask yourselves, "What do we value? What is our family all about? What do we stand for? What is our essential mission, our reason for being?"[1] On a bad day, full of whining and tears, these questions might be hard to contemplate. But maybe that is the best time to struggle with the answers. Covey reminds us, "If you want to get

anywhere long-term, identify core values and goals and get
the system aligned with these values and goals. Work on the
foundation. Make it secure. The core of any family is what
is changeless, what is always going to be there."[2]

An example of a family mission statement can be found
in The Covey Leadership Center's *Personal Leadership Application Workbook*. It reads as follows: "Our Family Mission—To love each other . . . To help each other . . . To
believe in each other . . . To wisely use our time, talents,
and resources to bless others . . . To worship together . . .
Forever."[3]

The diapers, the colic, and the grape juice spilled on the
rug will pass all too quickly. Think about why you and
your husband got together in the first place. Where will
you be, as a couple, when the children are gone? Will clar-
ifying and memorializing some of these values help you
through the hard times and help you to pass these values
on to your children? We think so. We have started teaching our four-year-old to recite our mission statement from
memory. Our children know we love them, but we also
want them to know why we are together as a family. We
believe this mission statement helps convey some very important ideals to our children.

Discussing the questions above as a couple (if your children are young) or as a family is the best way to begin defin-
ing your mission statement. Another helpful idea is to ask
where you would like to see your family be in five years, or
in ten years. What are the character traits you want to see
developed in your children? Then ask the follow-up question: How do we reach those goals?

Each day is another God-given opportunity to mold and
shape your children and to create an atmosphere in your
home. What important things do you want to teach them?
What should that atmosphere be like?

My Husband/My Partner

When I was able to set aside my ego and stop taking the pulse of the power relationship in our marriage, my husband and I became deeper friends.

"Once most women adjust to the new lifestyle of homemaking, both they and their husbands are pleasantly surprised at how much the change has helped to improve their relationship. Most men when interviewed freely admit that they are happiest when their wives are satisfied and at peace with themselves," says author Pamela Piljac.[4]

What do you enjoy most about being home?

Being able to be more single-minded in caring for my family.

—Jana Trovato

I also believe that most women are happiest when they know their husband is happy. Cheryl Ammons notes that "an involved husband makes staying at home a joy." Barbara Trudel says, "I am very fortunate to have an extremely supportive husband. It's a wonderful thing to find your one true love and share your life with him. He not only supports my decision to stay home, he encourages it. He also readily admits that having the kids and me to come home to is one of the things that helps him get through his own hard days at work."

Author D. Ross Campbell wrote a book to help us really love our children, but he also talks a great deal about husbands and wives loving each other. He says, "The most important relationship in the family is the marital relationship. It takes primacy over all others including the parent-child relationship. Both the quality of the parent-child bond and the child's security are largely dependent on the quality of the marital bond. So you can see why it is important to assure the best possible relationship between wife and husband before seriously attempting to relate to our child in more positive ways."[5] If mom and dad are in harmony, they set the tone for the whole family.

The healthiest marriages are the ones where each partner is committed—both to seeing the other grow and giving the energy to build the other up. Therefore, "Do not let any unwholesome talk come out of your mouths, but only what is helpful for building others up according to their needs, that it may benefit those who listen" (Eph. 4:29). Once again, wisdom from the Bible—the first and best manual ever written on marriage and family life.

Author Donna Otto tells the story of a stormy fight she had once with her husband. Although the underlying issue remained unresolved, he walked across the room to her and said, "Just remember: I am committed to you."[6] No matter how rocky the seas you may be negotiating in your relationship, remember to verbalize your commitment to love one another.

Sometimes the week goes by in a blur. Before I know it, it's Friday night, and I realize I have only exchanged a few sentences with my husband that week. A warning light goes off because we don't know what has gone on all week with the other person and we miss each other! It is a sad commentary indeed to miss the person you live with, the person who is dearest to your heart. But if your Friday night finds you sitting next to a stranger—your husband—it's time to reexamine, simplify, and reconnect.

I've seen more books written about marriage than I've seen diaper rashes. You can find lots of advice. But remember God guided you to your spouse in the first place. God made you partners before you were parents. God inspired the writing of the Bible, which can guide you in all your relationships. You can love your children with all your heart, but don't neglect your primary relationship with your husband. He won your heart first, well before the little ones came along.

You've heard it a million times: You have to make time for each other. Make a date night. Stay up after the kids are in bed. If money is tight, have a sitter exchange with neighbors or friends. Time alone with your husband doesn't have to be elaborate. My husband and I have had great conversations over a simple cup of coffee. Once we did grocery shopping together at the tail end of a date and had a marvelous time in the supermarket, chatting up and down the aisles. The most important thing to do is to reconnect with your spouse each day. Don't let the day go by when your only communication is a few informational questions and a few grunted answers.

The end of the day is usually the time when most families communicate. But there is a reason why they call dinner time the arsenic hour. The kids are hungry, and you and your spouse are tired from your long days. Ruth Gibson, author, counselor, and Wheaton M.O.P.S. (Mothers of Preschoolers) mentor, tells her moms that the end of the day is like merging traffic. "You have to merge gently with your spouse and be especially gentle with each other at the end of the day," she says. She reminds us that, "We can't have a *perfect* marriage, but we can have *this* one." She also cautions us to not let our feelings dictate our behavior. At the end of the day you may be mad at your children, mad at the world, or just feeling bad, but she encourages us to "step out on faith and do an act of love" for our spouse, even though we may not *feel* like doing it. The seeds of love and optimism we sow in the worst moments will bear the greatest fruit.

For some families, an act of love is letting Dad have a few minutes in the bedroom to change clothes and read the mail before he gets the daily update from you and the kids. In our family, because our children are small, it means starting them on dinner so Daddy can miss all the pre-dinner whining and fighting. (If they're feeding their hungry faces, they can't whine at the same time.)

My husband recently paid me a high compliment when he told me that our home feels like a haven for him. When he is having a tough day, he looks forward to coming home and the thought of home helps him through. I have intentionally tried to foster that feeling in our home for my husband and our children. I want home to be a place that helps people feel good and loved, a place where they can find healing and rest. So we attend to the special things that make up a home. One special part is respecting each other as unique individuals with unique needs and personalities. We are loved for *all* that we are, not just the pleasing, good parts. We are loved when we come home in a lousy mood or after a bad day. We are soothed by our homecoming, so we can be rejuvenated and slowly merged back into a family unit. A large part of my job as a mother at home is to foster and nurture that atmosphere for my family.

Counselor and author John Bradshaw sees the family as a system that is held in a delicate balance. When something upsets that balance (like the birth of children), a new equilibrium must be found. A healthy, functional relationship, according to Bradshaw, is a decision. It's an act of will based on unconditional love. It is not strictly a matter of shifting, changing feelings. When people in a healthy relationship decide to have children, they must realize that this is the most responsible decision of their lives, and they must commit to being there for their children. But there must also be a wholeness in Mom and in Dad, and they must recognize the primacy of their marriage relationship rather than pouring *all* their spiritual and physical energy into the children. "As long as Mom and Dad satisfy their own needs through their own powers and with each other," Bradshaw says, "they will not use the children to solve these needs." The result is an all-around healthier family.[7]

As difficult as it is for a dedicated mother to accept, your relationship with your husband requires just as much work as your relationship with your children. Where do you get the energy or time? Narrow the stream. Concentrate the efforts. Cut corners in cleaning and cooking. Say no to extraneous commitments. You were partners before you were parents, and marriage is not just about parenting.

Want to unlock romance? "Friendship is the key," says writer Angela Elwell Hunt. "Intimate friendship is the key to unlocking the romance that's been buried in the routine of your marriage. . . . Decide to become your spouse's best friend whether or not you get an immediate response."[8] How does a best friend act? They're interested; they listen; they respect differences; they make the effort. You may not be fascinated by your husband's stories about work, but let's face it, he's probably not thrilled to hear all the details of your day at home either. But you listen, you react, you support, and you encourage out of respect for the relationship and the person.

Love for the Long Haul

What if you're not feeling particularly friendly towards your spouse? Your unmet needs and unresolved differences can cause bitterness and resentment to grow in your heart. There is no better remedy for bitterness than gratitude. Have you thought about your husband's good qualities lately? If you are feeling discouraged, I encourage you to sit down to make a list of the ten things you are most grateful to your husband for. Certainly some of the things may be the daily contributions he makes, such as taking out the trash and bringing home a paycheck, but look a little deeper. Are you grateful for his sense of humor? Are you grateful that he is a godly man? Write these things down now, and see if they help you begin to look at your husband in a different light.

Things I Appreciate about My Husband

1.
2.
3.
4.
5.
6.
7.
8.
9.
10.

Review this list and ask yourself, "How do I *show* him that I appreciate these things?" If you don't show him, he may not know what you appreciate about him. He also may not know how to express his appreciation for you, so you will have to show him how. Instead of complaining and trying to change him yourself, set an example, turn it over to God, and pray for your husband.

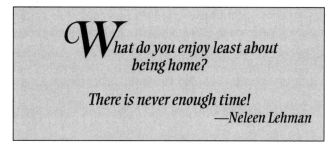

What do you enjoy least about being home?

There is never enough time!
—Neleen Lehman

It may also be helpful for you to take a look at what you expect from your husband. Sometimes I expect *too* much from my husband. I expect him to be my best friend, my lover, and my provider and to understand and anticipate everything I am thinking about or worried about. But the longer I am married, the more I realize that I need to give him a break. He is not a mind reader; he has faults, and he gets tired, too.

In the space below, make a list of the needs you expect your husband to fill for you. Are they realistic? In no way am I suggesting that a neglectful husband should be let off the hook. Rather, I am encouraging you to look at whether your expectations are reasonable.

Things I Expect from My Husband

1.
2.
3.
4.
5.
6.
7.
8.
9.
10.

After you make this list, put a check mark next to the needs that you are currently trying to meet for *him*. If you aren't making an effort to meet his needs, is it fair to expect him to meet all of yours?

Remember that you can never directly change another person. But you can try to change yourself, set a good example, and pray about the rest.

Taking Meals Together

It is a sad fact that many families rarely sit at the table together. Soccer practice, ballet lessons, part-time jobs, odd work schedules, and a million other distractions combine to keep us from eating together. Yet I believe that coming together at the table can strengthen our commitment and communication. If you can commit to sitting down for at least one meal a day together, you will have time to reconnect and share with all the members of your family.

Mealtime seems to be a natural time to connect, pray, and read from the Bible. It is a predictable break in the day, and using this time together for devotions can strengthen your family life. I wish I could say that we regularly do family devotions. However, they are a bit sporadic. I usually read the kids' Sunday school papers or do something from a devotional for preschoolers most days, but not every day. Around Easter and Christmas, we do special family devotions when Daddy comes home so he can read the Bible passage.

A recent 50-Day Spiritual Adventure (Chapel of the Air Ministries, Wheaton, Ill.) challenged participants to keep a list of "God hunt sightings"—evidence of God's work in the world. One family at my church has been doing this for years. They have several spiral notebooks filled with notations, and it is exciting for them to read through a notebook at dinnertime and remember answered prayer and past praises.

Our children are a bit young for this yet, but we like to ask them at dinner, "Tell us something good that happened today." If they can't remember, we remind them of something, and it gives us all a chance to review the day. A special delight is when they can rattle off three or four good things that happened, because we are assured that they are indeed counting their blessings.

If your schedule doesn't permit dinner together, how about breakfast or lunch? Try to carve out a predictable, reliable time to meet as a family each day. If you can read the Bible or a devotional during that time, all the better. You will be building traditions and instilling values in your children.

9

Finding Other Support

While the support of your husband and family is very important, connecting with other stay-at-home moms will give you the support your family can't provide. They will be friends for you to talk to who struggle with the same problems you have, who understand your needs and share your passions, and who can offer you encouragement, advice, and help when you need it. Here are some ideas for finding other stay-at-home moms and building your support group.

Support Organizations

F. E.M.A.L.E.—Formerly Employed Mothers at the Leading Edge

In 1987, Joanne Brundage founded F.E.M.A.L.E., previously named Formerly Employed Mothers at Loose Ends, because she recognized that the needs and problems she had as a newly-at-home mom—isolation, loss of self-esteem, loss of identity, and financial insecurity—were the same as others were facing. She felt these moms could help each other.

"I used to sit on park benches and look for other moms to try to start up a conversation," says Fiona Gierzynski, long-time F. E.M.A.L.E. member and mother of four. "Sometimes I would come home and cry to my husband because no one wanted to talk to me." Then four years ago, this former food broker joined her local chapter of F. E.M.A.L.E., which has brought richness and friendship to her experience of being an at-home mother.

F. E.M.A.L.E. is both a support and advocacy group, but seeks first to provide support to mothers at home. Many members view their time at home raising children as just one phase in their lives and wish to make the most of the experience. F. E.M.A.L.E. currently has worldwide membership of women from all facets of the working world who come together to share the joys and difficulties of their new role. They recently reached the milestone of one hundred local chapters that help women find other moms who are like-minded and who support their choices and priorities.

But F.E.M.A.L.E. also reaches beyond being just a support group. Because more women are choosing to balance career and family, F. E.M.A.L.E. also seeks to encourage business and government to become more responsive to the changing American family by making job-sharing, flex-time, on-site day care, and extended parental leave options more available.

Other member benefits include a monthly newsletter to help women learn about others who are modifying their work patterns and to keep them informed about the issues and events that concern today's families. Local chapters also feature play groups, baby-sitting co-ops, mom's-night-out activities, mom and tot activities, and an organized support system for times of personal need.

To find out if a chapter exists in your area or to inquire about starting a group, contact F. E.M.A.L.E. at the following address:

F. E.M.A.L.E.
P.O. Box 31
Elmhurst, IL 60126
(708) 941-3553

M.O.P.S.—Mothers of Preschoolers

It took me a year at home to get around to discovering our local M.O.P.S. group, but I wish I had found it sooner. M.O.P.S. was founded in 1973 as a program for mothers with children under school age. The group attracts a wide variety of women of all ages and backgrounds, but all trying to do a good job of mothering young children.

Local groups feature a children's program (MOPPETS) with caring teachers who usually provide a snack, craft, songs, and stories for the children. The activities are all biblically based, and children really love the morning. Each chapter has a mentor, usually an experienced mother, who speaks to the group about their roles as mother, wife, and woman. My chapter is fortunate enough to have author and counselor Ruth Gibson. She has the uncanny ability to speak to the issues most heavy on our hearts and is an inspiration and encouragement to us. When time permits, the larger group breaks up into smaller groups to discuss a topic or just share feelings.

Each session also features a simple craft project, the cost of which is included in the fee paid for each visit. The project is designed to be completed at the meeting—for those of us who can't focus our attention for more than thirty seconds at home without interruption.

M.O.P.S. boasts a national membership of thirty thousand in some seven hundred groups across the country. It fills a real need for mothers at home in our society as Elisa Morgan, president of M.O.P.S. International, noted in a recent interview: "Moms seem to have less certainty about themselves, their identity, their competency as mothers. There are a myriad of options available about what we can do with our lives and the gifts God has given us, but not many role models who can show us how to juggle all these opportunities. Finding a healthy balance between all these possibilities is our biggest challenge."[1] M.O.P.S. can be a real help in this process.

If you would like to join or start a M.O.P.S. program in your area, they may be contacted at the following address:

> M.O.P.S. International, Inc.
> 1311 S. Clarkson
> Denver, CO 80210
> (303) 733-5353

Mothers at Home, Inc.

Mothers at Home, Inc., publishes a monthly magazine called *Welcome Home* that is worth its weight in gold. The group was founded in 1984 with the mission of providing support for women through the pages of a magazine. *Welcome Home* is not a traditional women's magazine. There are no ads for hair coloring or diapers. In fact, there are no ads at all. But there are lots of articles to warm your heart and make you want to go hug your children. Each month, this little publication provides a wealth of encouragement through articles written by moms just like you who are going through some of the same things you go through with your family. I look forward to receiving each issue and savor it every month.

Current subscriptions are eighteen dollars per year, and can be purchased by writing to the address below:

> Mothers at Home, Inc.
> 8310A Old Courthouse Road
> Vienna, VA 22182

M.O.M.S.—Moms Offering Moms Support

This nationwide group had its start in California in 1983 and currently has about fifty chapters. They offer monthly meetings, play groups and outings, and social activities for all mothers with children of all ages, not just preschoolers. They may be contacted at the following address:

The National M.O.M.S. Club
814 Moffatt Circle
Simi Valley, CA 93065
(805) 526-2725

Doulas of North America

Doulas are not midwives, and they do not provide medical care. Rather, they are childbirth assistants who provide supportive companionship, labor coaching if needed, and knowledge. The term comes from the ancient Greek language. In earlier times, doulas were women servants in the household who helped the women of the house through childbearing.

"Doulas also give emotional, physical and informational support to women before and after birth. In fact, there are some doulas, known as postpartum doulas, whose function is to help the woman and family only after birth," notes a recent article in the *Wheaton Journal*.[2]

I didn't hear about doulas until after my new parenthood crisis had passed. I wish I had heard before! But now one of my life goals is to find someone I can be a doula for.

Doulas have been practicing in California for about ten years, and are now beginning to practice around the country. For information about doulas or about becoming a doula, write (or fax) to the following address:

Doulas of North America (DONA)
1100 23rd Avenue East
Seattle, WA 98112
Fax: (206) 325-0472

La Leche League

La Leche League is the mother of all mother support groups. It has been around since 1956 and exists primarily to support the breast-feeding family. However, they also have materials available on a variety of other subjects. Informal monthly meetings are held just about everywhere in the country, and they also offer support through a bimonthly magazine called *New Beginnings.*

You may contact them at the following address:

> La Leche League International
> 1400 N. Meacham Rd.
> P.O. Box 4079
> Schaumburg, IL 60168-4079
> 1-800-LALECHE or (708) 455-7730

Newcomers Groups

Does your area have a newcomers group? This is a social group designed specifically for people who are new to an area. They have coffees and meetings where you can meet other couples in the same position—people who are new to an area and are learning their way around like you. Members can receive advice on shopping, finding a doctor, or the hundreds of other questions a new resident may have. To locate a newcomers group, look in the phone book under "Associations and Clubs," or contact your Chamber of Commerce.

Play Groups

A play group can be a wonderful experience for both mother and child. It can be either a social gathering for mothers or a structured, directed playtime for the children. For younger children, the group will generally be the former. Some people say that a play group for younger children is a waste of time because children under two don't play together. They may play beside one another, but not with one another. However, don't underestimate the value of spending that time with other moms. You can put the babies on the floor, have a few minutes for a cup of coffee, and trade mothering stories.

For children two or older, the group can be as elaborate or as simple as the participants want. Older children can make new friends in a play group and share toys and experiences. The simplest form is one where the sponsoring mom provides the coffee and the space and the guests bring snacks and kids. The kids can watch a video or have their dolls trade clothing. Meanwhile, the moms may be gaining a new perspective by this respite.

How do you find other moms for a play group? The best way (and the most convenient) is to form a play group with your neighbors. Spread the word around or circulate a flyer. Bring it up during the summer when people are on their porches. Plan ahead for the winter days when your houses are sealed and your neighbors seem miles away.

Another way to discover a play group is through support groups or other parent groups. One of the many benefits of joining such a group is the chance to plug into a play group. Some groups, like Formerly Employed Mothers at the Leading Edge (F.E.M.A.L.E.) or Preschool PTAs, have an organized referral system. Most F.E.M.A.L.E. chapters try to match their members by ages of children and geographic areas. If you don't have a F.E.M.A.L.E. chapter or other support group, you can circulate the word at your church and perhaps put a notice on a message board or in the bulletin.

One ambitious group of women in my area took this idea and ran with it. Called Mom and Tots, they use space donated by the Lutheran Church of the Master in Carol Stream, Illinois, and have a different group meeting each day of the week with a separate contact person organizing each day. The groups meet for an hour and a half with a maximum of twenty-five kids in each group. They charge a five dollar per month fee per family to cover the cost of arts and crafts. Activities include a circle time with songs and finger plays, an arts and crafts session, a large motor activity, a snack time with a story or two, and a free playtime when the moms have a chance to visit with one another.

In this highly organized group, each mom contributes to the workload by signing up to be responsible for an activity for one month, and everyone benefits. The snack mom brings the goodies and chooses the stories. The circle-time mom comes up with the songs and finger plays. The arts-and-crafts mom decides on the craft and secures the materials for the month. The group is lots of fun, well run, and well attended. They attract new members by running free public service ads in local and regional newspapers.

Getting to Know Your Neighbors

I have met many women who live in neighborhoods that literally empty out in the morning and are repopulated with parents and children at dinnertime. God was clearly watching out for us when he chose our house for us. In many ways, it is inadequate for our needs, but we have great neighbors with lots of kids, a big fenced yard, and a gorgeous maple tree in front.

We moved in July, so the process of getting to know our neighbors was easier. Everyone in our neighborhood is out in the summer. The moms and dads with older kids have the luxury of sitting in lawn chairs. The rest of us do a lot of chasing and shepherding.

One of the best ways to get to know your neighbors is by simply being available. We can't send our small children out to play alone, so we all go out together. We cherish our side-walk chalk drawings and always have extra pieces of chalk for other children. When we have tea parties in the grass, we have an extra cup. With lots of outside toys, your house will attract other children. If your kids are doing bubbles, have an extra bottle or an extra wand in case another child wants to join in.

In the natural process of living with and playing with your children, you will meet your neighbors and hopefully forge some deep friendships. It has been such a blessing for us to have someone to call in an emergency and to have friends to trade occasional baby-sitting.

*W*hat do you enjoy most about being home?

Freedom (in a relative sense), watching Elizabeth unfold and blossom, peace, quiet, family time in the evening, and more time for family and friends.

—Cynthia McCabe

A Recipe for an Inexpensive, Super Block Party

During the second summer in our house, we organized a block party. A few neighbors had mentioned it, so we took the initiative to organize it, even though we were among the newer residents. The temperature that day was close to one hundred degrees, but we had a marvelous time.

- *Ingredient 1:* To begin, we passed around two flyers— one about a month before and another about a week and a half before the party. The neighbors got the news early enough to plan and then got a reminder.
- *Ingredient 2:* We told each family to bring their own meat, chairs, and one dish to pass. We had two grills fired up and a large picnic table. We also provided cups, plates, and pop, although most people brought their own as well.
- *Ingredient 3:* We designated grill-masters—my husband and another neighbor.
- *Ingredient 4:* We turned on our lawn sprinkler and filled a couple of small wading pools. We also had water balloons and a backyard spigot for filling them.

- *Ingredient 5:* We bought several small gifts from the dollar store. The children wrote their names on pieces of paper and put them in a box. When their name was drawn, they got to pick a small prize. It was inexpensive and non-competitive and each child went home with something.
- *Ingredient 6:* We had lots of sidewalk chalk, and the kids drew some wonderful stuff. We also had tape and streamers so all the children could decorate their bikes or ride-on toys, and we had our own little parade.
- *Ingredient 7:* One mom organized a few simple games: improvised Bozo buckets, ring toss, hiding pennies in some tall grass for the little ones to find, tag, and drop the clothespin in the bottle.

In many areas, the local police, fire, or forest preserve district will visit your block party. You may arrange for a police car, a fire truck, or a police officer on horseback. They answer the children's questions, and everyone loves the chance to look at police and fire stuff.

You might also want to take a group photo or photos of the kids. Later you can make lots of copies and deliver them to the neighbors to keep the friendships growing.

In her book, *Family Traditions,* author Elizabeth Berg mentions another great suggestion for your block party—have a junk exchange! Tell people to bring something that's still good but that they don't want anymore. Some suggestions are books, cookware, toys, and knickknacks. Designate an area to place the items, and make each person who brings an item take one home. This is a great way to trade and share some items with your neighbors.[3]

Friendship Basket

But what if it is the middle of winter, your grill is in the deep freeze, and you still want to get to know your neighbors? Gloria Gaither and Shirley Dobson have a wonderful idea in their book, *Let's Make a Memory*.[4] Make and pass a traveling friendship basket. Get a nice-sized basket and fill it with some special treats. Decorate the basket with pretty ribbons or flowers and include a note asking the receiving neighbor to fill it with their own goodies and pass the basket to the neighbor on the other side of them.

The ideas for the contents of the basket are limited only by your imagination. You can buy or bake, add flowers or a small, handmade item. At Christmas time, you can add a homemade ornament. Be creative and share some of your blessings with your neighbors!

Other Ideas

There are so many ways neighbors can support and enjoy one another. When you're making a trip to the store, you can ask your neighbor if she needs something, especially if you're traveling to a discount warehouse. You can also save coupons or watch the sales for one another.

How about a neighborhood exercise group? Some of my neighbors meet regularly most mornings at 8 A.M. to watch (and do!) an exercise show. Their kids play together while the moms get some exercise—and no one has to pay a hefty health club fee.

Other neighbors have organized toy exchanges. Each family brings an agreed number of items and can trade for an equal number of different toys. Exchanges can also be done with clothing.

Author Marilee Horton has a theory, "perhaps unscientific, that psychiatrists' couches are filled with people who could have been cured by 'under the maple tree' therapy. . . . Millions of dollars being spent for professional counseling could just as well be saved if we had some neighbors practicing the ancient art of listening in the backyard. . . . Each person has a particular spot to fill in our lives, but working sometimes jams the slots with 'Occupied' signs and our neighbors fade away into the clouds of busy activity."[5]

Your neighbors can be a tremendous source of friendship and support. It is worth the time and effort to get to know them.

Support from Your Church

The February 1994 issue of *Moody Monthly* was dedicated to moms at home and included articles that encouraged churches to view moms at home as a growing field for ministry. Churches can play a vital role in helping women who are newly at home to navigate the waters of isolation and loneliness and can provide a Christian outreach to non-Christian mothers.

Author Karen Moderow makes specific suggestions on how a congregation can address the physical and spiritual needs of stay-at-home moms. "Begin with baby," she says, noting that child care may be what draws a tired mom to church for nurturing.[6] Having quality care in place is vital for attracting families to church. She also suggests considering a day care ministry, or a place where a mother can leave her children a few hours a week at no charge. Some churches host "Mother's Day Out" programs, but they often charge a monthly fee which may be prohibitive for many mothers. If a church cannot afford these ministries, perhaps they can coordinate a baby-sitting co-op to provide the same benefit for mothers.

M.O.P.S. (Mothers of Preschoolers) works in conjunction with a local church. If your church does not have a chapter, maybe you can be the one to organize it! However, if your church is small, a more informal group where mothers can meet, rest, and share can be just as effective.

Churches can also make themselves inviting to moms by offering courses or seminars of interest to parents, such as two-year-old discipline or potty training. They can also create a mother's network to link mothers up with other mothers who can help them with specific problems. (A woman in our church is my potty training prayer warrior. Her prayers have helped each of our children potty train.)

> *What do you enjoy least about being home?*
>
> *Trying to manage a restaurant without a license, trying to keep the house clean while I have two little house-wreckers running around, and trying to keep my emotions cool when I'm ready to blow my top.*
> *—Laura Englehart*

Finally, a church can facilitate and encourage Titus 2 relationships between women, such as a mentoring friendship between a spiritually mature mother and a struggling mom who wants to grow spiritually. For example, our church has a ministry called "Heart to Heart" that matches up women who are seeking this type of arrangement. Mother-at-home Caron LaPlante says, "I rely on God to give me strength and peace in my daily routines. Talking to other mothers who also have a strong faith in God is encouraging."

If you feel called to a personal ministry to other moms in need, there is no better place to start than your own church.

10

Getting It All Done

Which would you rather do: spend fifteen minutes searching for a little-used pressure cooker, or spend that fifteen minutes doing something fun with your children?

I used to bristle at the notion that by taking time to organize for efficiency I could *save* time in the long run. I was doing just fine in the midst of my clutter and disarray, thank you. But with each succeeding child with their multiple, varied needs, I began to realize the value of organizing and planning ahead. The initial investment of time to organize paid a dividend of liberation from disorganization—a freeing of time to be used in more exciting ways.

Take one small step today to get a handle on organizing your home life. Clean out one drawer. Work your way up to organizing the (gulp) garage. Here are some ways to get started.

Getting Organized: The Dreaded Kitchen

I have a tiny kitchen in which I do many things. It is not only cooking central, it is also our craft area and has seen the baking and decorating of many, many cookies. It is far from perfect and is not my dream kitchen, but it is the one I have to work with.

I have to have an emotional attachment to my kitchen because I spend so much time there. I want to make it aesthetically pleasing with bright colors and homey touches, but it also must be organized so I can work there most efficiently. Let's look at some ideas for organization.

Physical Organization for Efficiency

Deniece Schofield is a home organization expert. In her book, *Escape From the Kitchen*, she suggests looking at your kitchen as a series of work centers and storing items at their point of first use.[1] The kitchen centers are a sink center (where you wash but also peel), the cooking center (where you also store pots and pans), the mixing center (a preparation area where you get things ready to eat and store ingredients), the serving center (more for a larger kitchen), and the refrigerator center. It makes sense to store things where they will be used to save time as well as steps.

For example, Norma Kunda divides her spices up, placing the ones to season foods during cooking near the stove. The spices and other items for baking are on the other end of the kitchen in her mixing area. "This meant keeping salt and measuring spoons in two places," she says, "but this saves running back and forth." If you cook every day, or cook in any kind of volume, a few minutes spent thinking about the organizational pattern of your kitchen can save you some time in the long run.

And of course, any discussion of physical organization must include a discussion of clutter. Deniece Schofield, in *Confessions of a Happily Organized Family*, says, "Clutter is a parasite. It receives food and shelter at your expense and multiplies faster than fruit flies around a ripe banana."[2] Does that sound like those five hundred margarine tubs in your cabinet? Seems like only yesterday there were only two . . .

Deniece has a clutter checklist that could be used in any room in your house, but is especially helpful in your kitchen. She advises giving away or selling: (1) anything you haven't used for one year or more; (2) things you dislike and don't want, but that are too good to just throw in the trash; (3) things you have no current use for, even though they might come in handy someday (when was the last time you served fondue?); (4) things you didn't remember you had; or (5) things you haven't missed and haven't been looking for. If you honestly evaluate the items bulging from your cabinets, many will not escape this scrutiny. Remember, less clutter is more space and a simplified kitchen.

I knew I had a cabinet-clutter problem when our daughter was sitting on the floor taking off her shoes, and when I opened the cabinet above her to get some soup, a can fell out, narrowly missing her sweet little head. That was my inspiration to spring clean the cabinets, and I boxed up several items to give away. I haven't missed a single item, and my cabinets have room to spare. The kitchen looks neater and is easier to maintain because I am not continually looking for space in which to cram things.

Children in the Kitchen

When our children were too small to actually help, it was a great challenge to keep them busy in the kitchen while I cooked. Children want to be with you. They want to watch and help. What a marvelous opportunity to teach some skills and share some special time!

We came up with some creative solutions for our small children, as have some other moms. At our house, the girls have two drawers in the cabinets that are theirs. They can keep dolls, plastic toys, anything they want in them. This drawer of goodies usually kept them occupied for a few minutes at a time.

Laura Englehart says, "My unbreakable, entertaining baking pans and kitchen items are in a lower cabinet with a lock so I can open it for grande entertainment as I choose." She also says, "I learned that I could be saved from thirty to forty seconds of tears or questions from a youngster waiting for juice if I sent him for the cup while I wrestled in the refrigerator for the juice. So my plastic cups are down low." Smart lady!

What can an older child do? Look at the simple skills that your child can use to make him or her feel important in the kitchen: stirring, measuring, cracking eggs, washing up, or cutting with an appropriate knife. It will inevitably slow you down to let your child participate in the kitchen, but I think it's worthwhile.

Menu Planning, Cooking, and Shopping

How many times have you scanned the cupboards and refrigerator thinking, "Hmmm, what sounds good for supper tonight?" If you do it once in a while, you're okay. But if you do it every meal every day, you're in trouble!

I used to think I didn't have time to plan menus. Now I realize I don't have time not to plan them. Planning saves time on the actual shopping trip because you know what you're looking for, and it also saves added trips to the store during the week because you forgot something. Planning also saves money because you'll buy just what you need, and you'll be able to take advantage of sales and specials when you scan your weekly newspapers. And planning will enable you to prepare some tag-along meals and relieve some of your stress and time in the kitchen.

Are you convinced yet? Well, dig out your cookbooks, because that's where you start. I have about twenty-five cookbooks. I know women who collect them and have over one hundred. Do you use all your cookbooks? How can you use them more efficiently? Lori Solyom says to keep a bookshelf in your kitchen for all your cookbooks. She also keeps a wall-paper-covered box with file folders for all the recipes she clips—her giant recipe box.

If you really want to organize your menu planning, find the recipes you use most often, along with those you would like to see incorporated into your regular routine. Then copy them (or photocopy them) so they are all in one place—a recipe box or a notebook or whatever suits your organizational style. After you put together this mother-lode of recipe ideas, sit down and select recipes for a week or two. Build your shopping list off of this plan and you will have supper organized. Believe it or not, you will actually save time by not having to think about menus every day. Pull out the recipes in the evening for the next day's fare and check ingredients. You can begin defrosting meat and other frozen items to be ready to go for the next day.

What about breakfast and lunch? These tend to be repetitive and spontaneous—that is, we eat the same things over and over, but we don't decide what to eat until the last possible minute. You know your family's favorites. You might also have some other items you would like to rotate into your diet. But when you're pressed for time and have fifteen other things on your mind, you may not come up with the best choices. I find that if I have the options written out and visible, I am more likely to make a healthy choice.

Make a chart for the front of your refrigerator that has sample breakfasts, lunches, and snacks. Yours might look like this:

Breakfasts

boiled egg	cereal	grapefruit
toast	banana	English muffin
orange juice	milk	with jelly
		juice

oatmeal
raisins
toast
juice or milk

fruit
bagel with jelly
juice or milk

Lunches

cottage cheese
fruit
bagel

chicken breast
  on pita
  bread
lettuce and
  tomato
fruit

soup
cheese
apple

salad
fruit
raw vegs

turkey on pita
raw vegs
fruit

soup
fruit
rice cakes

tuna on bagel
tomato slices
fruit

Snacks

yogurt
pita chips
crackers
raw vegs
tomato juice

fruit
popcorn
cheese
rice cakes
ginger snaps

graham
  crackers
pretzels
fruit juice
  w/seltzer
low fat cookies

If you want to plan an exact menu for the week to stream-
line your shopping, fill out a simple menu planner like the

one below. Then use the menu planner to make out an exact shopping list.

	Breakfast	Snacks	Lunch	Dinner
Monday				
Tuesday				
Wednesday				
Thursday				
Friday				
Saturday				
Sunday				

Something else to consider to aid your menu planning are the food sales ads in newspapers. Donna Pindel says she plans her entire menu around them. "Grocery shopping is my recreation, and I will shop the sales at three stores or more," she quips. In our area, several large grocery stores are all within a few blocks, so the use of gasoline is a minimal consideration. Donna saves money and gets some much-needed time alone. She says, "Since the birth of my third child, I usually shop at night while my husband baby-sits." More than one mom advises, "Never bring children!" If you have to bring them, bring a cookie or snack with you to keep them entertained and avoid some of the gimmies.

Debbie Wilcoxen, whose children are a little older than mine, involves the whole family in menu planning. She says, "I ask each person in the family to list three meals for the next two weeks. It can't be going out to eat or ordering pizza. That way, everyone gets at least three of their favorite meals."

Lori Solyom says, "After several years of haphazard-style menu planning, I know what my family enjoys and what they will eat so my menu planning is very easy." She has a "Food of the Day" for every day of the week and builds her menus around these foods. Monday is pasta; Tuesday is chicken; Wednesday is potatoes or eggs; Thursday is tuna; Friday is pizza (homemade, frozen, or delivered);

Saturday is sandwiches; and Sunday is casseroles, or "skip it and bring home bagels and spreads." With a selected main food for each day of the week, she can try any number of recipes with these foods as the starting point.

Or, you could take the easy route. Susan Fenton jokes that her top three tips for menu planning and shopping are McDonald's, Burger King, and Taco Bell.

Cooking Once a Month

If you want to be a truly organized cook, you might try cooking once a month. Mimi Wilson and Mary Beth Lagerborg, authors of *Once a Month Cooking*, have compiled an entire system for you to use should you decide to cook once every thirty days. The book has recipes and detailed instructions on what to chop and dice when and how to put it all together in the freezer. Mimi Wilson says that, "I developed this plan because I felt I had to do something drastic to squeeze more time into my day. I had three young children, a busy husband, and company two or three times a week. . . . I used time studies to determine where I wasted the most time, and I found it was in making meals from scratch each day. It's not as if I went to the garden every day or killed the chickens for dinner. Even so, I believed I could save significant time in the kitchen."[3] In their plan, they recommend shopping one day and cooking the next, because a month of meals will take an entire day or more to complete. But with one day of hard labor, you're home free for the rest of the month's dinners!

Another mega-cooking approach can be found in *Dinner's in the Freezer! More Mary and Less Martha: A Home Management System* by Jill Bond.[4] This book has several recipes that can be made in multiples and frozen. She also shows you how to multiply your own recipes to cut down your time in the kitchen. It makes a lot of sense—if you're going to do the work for one casserole, why not make three and freeze the others for another time? If you are not quite up for once-a-month cooking, this system might be for you. Like Marnie Murray says, "I always make large batches of stews, soups, or chili and freeze them. Then it's done!"

Even one simple modification can save you some time. Norma Kunda says, "Buy a lot of hamburger when the price drops to ninety-nine cents and fry it up ahead of time, then freeze the pre-cooked ground beef to use in a quick spaghetti/pasta dish, soup, hamburger and noodles, or as a pizza topping." Some women chop and cook up enough onions or celery to last for a month then freeze them in plastic bags in small amounts for individual meals.

Cooks' Co-op

Four moms in Illinois formed a cooks' co-op. They came up with a weekly schedule of main dishes: chicken, pork, beef, and a surprise. One mom would cook four chicken dinners, keep one for her family, and deliver the other three to the other women in the co-op. Another mom would cook four pork dinners, and so on. It has worked out amazingly well for them, cutting their cooking time from fifteen hours a week to three hours a week, even though they were preparing meals for four families. They had to discuss their likes and dislikes and came up with a list of no-nos (no fish or sauerkraut), but all are enjoying a more varied menu than any one would have alone, and their children are loving the adventure.[5]

A modified version of a cooks' co-op is practiced by Denise Wickline, a mom at home. She says, "When you prepare a favorite dish, make double and share half with a friend, already packaged and ready for freezing (the food, not the friends). If each of you does this periodically, you can help fill each other's freezers with fast meals for no-cook days."

How about a no-groceries week or a clean-out-the-cabinets week? Plan a week once in a while when you clean out the pantry and freezer, using up the food with improvised recipes. You may also find some favorites hiding in your cupboards that you can rely on in a pinch.

Food Co-ops

To save on your overall food budget, food co-ops are a wonderful resource. Groups of families come together to buy foods in bulk. They usually place a large order once a month and take turns working to divide it up when it arrives. This arrangement will help you plan because you only order once a month. The co-ops generally offer everything from groceries to herbs to health care products. You can find out about co-ops in your area through the National Co-op Directory's *A Guide to Cooperative Natural Food Retailers across the Country*, which has 270 listings and sells for four dollars. For a copy of the guide, send a check and a self-addressed, stamped envelope to the address below:

Co-op News Network
Box 583
Spencer, WV 25276

Tag-Along Menu Ideas

I *love* the concept of taking a day off from cooking. However, our budget and our health will not allow us to eat out every other day. So I came up with some ideas to prepare enough on one day to form the basis for another meal using what I call tag-along recipes:

- Prepare two batches of spaghetti sauce and two batches of noodles. Serve with salad and bread. Use the second batch of noodles to make cold pasta salad. Serve the second batch of sauce over rice and cheese.
- Prepare a stir fry with fresh vegetables and chicken and make two batches of brown rice. Use the second batch

of brown rice for a new breakfast idea—serve warmed with chopped apples, raisins, honey, or brown sugar.

- Prepare baked chicken, fresh broccoli, and two batches of couscous (Moroccan pasta in the rice section of your supermarket). Use the second batch of couscous to make a tuna salad with vegetables and salad dressing.
- Buy a whole, baked deli chicken and potato salad from your supermarket deli. Use chopped chicken leftovers to make a casserole with wild rice and mushrooms.

As you go over the meals you commonly prepare, be on the lookout for opportunities to stretch your preparation time by making extra of something to use in another dish. By using this method, you can have a few no-cooking days.

Food Budget-Cutting Tips

A new or used freezer or extra refrigerator can really help you cut your food budget. We received a freezer/refrigerator *free* from a friend and hauled it to our garage. It houses items I have bought or made in bulk and has saved us tons of money. I don't hesitate to make two or three extra casseroles because I know I have a place to freeze them. If a store has a fabulous sale on meat or frozen juice, I scoop it up because I have a place to store it.

What about coupons? The frugal zealot, Amy Dacyczyn, says, "Most of us have seen newspaper articles or television shows featuring coupon experts who demonstrate their skills by taking reporters shopping and buying $134.86 of groceries, but after all the coupons are subtracted pay only $54.73. This type of shopping trip requires months of planning, and it is not typical of these shoppers' usual trips to the store."[6] The frugal zealot recommends a mixed approach that includes coupons, refunding, gardening, bulk buying, and baking from scratch. Also, keep your eyes open for a store that features a double-coupon day. It could be worth driving a few extra miles to attend.

Brenda Passon, a mom at home, has a neat system for using coupons that has a built-in incentive to organize and use them wisely. She writes the check out for the full amount of her groceries, then gets cash back for her coupons. "I use that money for a trip to McDonald's with the kids or a treat for myself."

I don't like gimmicks or fancy appliances with limited uses, but a recent present from my husband that I use is a Kitchen Aid basic mixer. He had an ulterior motive in buying it for me because he loves fresh bread, and his scheming has worked. I bake fresh bread every week in a minimum of time. The mixer does the hard mixing, but the children and I still have the opportunity to do some kneading when we punch the bread down after the first rising. I use it for other recipes as well. I love it and plan to add attachments at some point, like a food processor. Suzanne Gardner says she gets a lot of mileage out of her rice cooker with steaming tray. "It's a great way to prepare an easy, healthy meal of rice and vegetables."

How often does your child eat an entire piece of fruit? Probably rarely, which means you usually throw most of your fresh fruit away. We save chunks of leftover fruit in the freezer to use later in milkshakes. Frozen pieces of banana, orange, apple, or grape are tasty when mixed in the blender with milk and yogurt. You can also try drying some fruit, which is cheaper than fresh because you can prepare and serve smaller portions. A fancy dehydrator will give you directions on how to dry most anything, but try some dried fruits before you buy one to see if your family will eat them. To dry apples, put peeled, thinly sliced apples on a rack in the oven at very low heat for four to five hours. You can dry bananas the same way, but it takes about twenty-four hours on very low heat.

Perpetual Shopping Lists

Caron LaPlante says, "I keep a list handy and write down items as I need them, so when I make up my list, I don't have to stand in the kitchen and try to remember what I need." Keeping a list will not only help you remember what you need but will also help keep you on your budget. Kelly Rudy says to also, "Use a calculator in the grocery store so when you get to the register, you won't be surprised by your bill."

There are a few different ways to keep a list. Some moms draft a list based on the layout of their store. But if you shop at more than one store, this list may be difficult to use. Also, the chain I shop moves everything around about every six months just to confuse us and keep shopping interesting, so I use a perpetual shopping list based on the departments in any grocery store. If you keep a copy of this list posted on the refrigerator or taped in a cabinet, you can fill in the specifics you need under each heading.

Shopping List

produce	baking goods
fruits	spices
vegetables	condiments
bakery	frozen foods
breads	convenience foods
cereals	household items
canned goods	health and beauty
meat	misc.
dairy	
milk	
cheese	
eggs	

Nonfood items can really send your food bill through the roof. The items listed below are best purchased at a discount store, because grocery store prices are generally much higher.

dish soap	trash bags
laundry soap	paper napkins
shampoo	paper towels
toothpaste	toilet paper
cosmetics	baby needs

What about buying generic? Most families have developed a taste preference for some items and will not eat generic brands. But many items you buy at the store have the same chemical makeup whether they are generic or brand name. You can save by buying the cheapest item, no matter what the label, for these products:

baking soda	cooking oil
cornstarch	dried fruit
extracts	herbs
honey	lemon, lime juice
molasses	powdered milk
orange juice	nuts
salt	spices
sugar	flour

Another mom, writing in *The Heart Has Its Own Reasons*, says that she relies on a list divided into three sections.[7] The first is essentials, the second are things that are needed but not strictly essential, and the third is odds and ends she'd like to have if there is enough money. Sometimes the nonessentials can wait for several weeks, and sometimes they are actually crossed off the list! If you have a problem with impulse shopping, this can be a good way to stop. Force yourself to wait a week before you buy something you think you need. Sometimes I completely forget about things that seemed to be urgent.

Lori Solyom writes her shopping list on used envelopes. "I slip in my meal plan for the week, which is written on 3 x 5 cards, then I slip in coupons and my allotted cash. These envelopes and lists hang on my fridge so I can easily add things."

Papers, Papers, Everywhere!

Papers that come into our house have a short life span. They have to find a home or they are gone. Considering just the volume of junk mail alone, if you didn't keep up with the papers in your life, they would get truly out of hand.

Danette Kaschalk, a mom at home, says she keeps a separate file folder for various categories of papers. For example, she has a file for church activities, school, Cub Scouts, and doctors. Adding to this theme, I have a file for each group I belong to so I know where to find a newsletter or check the date for an event. I also have a file called "think about." Into this file go flyers or ads for events or purchases that I need to think about before committing.

Lori Solyom, mom at home, has another neat organizer idea. She keeps a *go box.* "A plastic bin sits on a shelf and holds my purse, sunglasses, keys, and whatever needs to leave the house—a package to go to the post office, a video to be returned, and my Bible study book. There is also room on the shelf for a packed diaper bag and mini-totes for my bigger girls."

In my former profession, I had an office, a secretary, a dictating machine, state-of-the-art computers, and anything else needed for efficiency. I now have a blue plastic carton by the telephone to organize my life that my husband jokingly refers to as "my office." I prefer it this way.

Unending Laundry

How can such little people create so much laundry? While tiny babies go through laundry by merely exercising their bodily functions, toddlers and older kids create dirty clothes by painting and playing in mud. Early in my mothering career, I concluded that if our kids weren't tired and dirty at the end of the day, I hadn't done my job that day. Dirty clothes don't bother us around our house.

But I hate the idea of doing laundry every day. To do so detracts from my precious family time. Many a husband has remarked, "What's the big deal about throwing some clothes in the washer?" Well, it's not just throwing them in the washer. The time-consuming part is sorting, folding, and putting away. It doesn't make a whole lot of sense to me to go through those three steps for one load of laundry. You have to decide what suits the rhythm of your household, but why not try to arrange it so you do multiple loads once or twice a week?

Laundry Day

Some thirty years or more ago, my mother (who raised eight children) had an old-fashioned wringer-washer. She said it saved her money on detergent and water. I like the money-saving aspect, but I would hate to be tied down to a machine that required my attention every few minutes. My mother also hung laundry out to dry on a clothesline. I must confess that I begged my husband to install a clothesline in our yard. Every day I am grateful for my dryer, but on those bright, sunny, summery days, there is something peaceful and reassuring about hanging out a load of clothes. I like to dry sheets and towels on the line, and our children like to use it to construct tents for outside adventures and tea parties. Ruth Gibson, mother and author, also says, "Hang anything with elastic on a clothes line to dry, and it will last longer." A modern convenience can't replace everything.

To help with the laundry, I have a clothes basket in each child's room. (I got this idea from another mom-at-home, Jackie Wellwood.) They put the dirty clothes in the basket, and they are learning to put away their own clean clothing from the basket when it is returned. Another help for laundry, suggested by Marnie Murray, is keeping a "stain stick" in the bathroom cabinet. "That way," she says, "at bath time, we pre-treat the stains as the clothes come off, and they're easier to wash."

Start washing early in the day so you aren't still at it when the sun sets. Choose a laundry day when you'll be home pretty much all day doing other things. Jodi Tatum says, "I set aside Mondays as my laundry/cleaning day. I make no other plans for the day except to do laundry and clean and then I can forget about it for the rest of the week!"

Hang clothes up as soon as you remove them from the dryer to save ironing (ugh!) time. Try to stock up ironing so you can do it all at once. Also, sometimes a "dry clean only" item can get an extra wearing if you put it in the dryer on the air cycle with a fabric softener sheet and let it freshen up a bit. Pin socks together if you're really organized. Or keep a non-matching sock box. You'd be surprised how many eventually find mates.

Involve your kids as much as possible in happy anticipation of the day when they can do the laundry themselves. Even the youngest children can sort dark from light colors, and learning to fold towels can become an exciting, athletic event. Let them do it. They want to belong and feel needed. Other things they can do to help are to pour the soap into the machine, load clothes into the dryer, close the dryer door, and push buttons. Given a playful, fun attitude, laundry day can be a learning, close time with your children.

Finally, Karen Gresk says, "Remember there will *always* be dirty laundry and cleaning to be done." Try to do it efficiently so you have the time and the energy for the important stuff.

Buying Clothes for Children

In order to keep on this once-a-week laundry schedule, you have to have enough clothes to last, but not so many that you don't have room to store them. Try to de-emphasize clothes with your children. If your kids have too much clothing, it gets stuffed into drawers and closets and makes more work for mom. And do they really need more than a week's worth of outfits?

> *What do you enjoy most about being home?*
>
> *Having direct input into helping my children develop, being there for them, and enjoying the simple, everyday experiences with them.*
> —Neleen Lehman

Prior to the beginning of each season, I go through all the old clothes and make a list of clothing needed for each child. I note the item and the size and keep the list in my purse. Then I'm ready to take advantage of any buying opportunity.

I rarely buy new items of clothing for our children. And I do not have the gift of sewing, so I have had to be creative about building their wardrobes. I have been fortunate enough to use garage and clothing sales to obtain almost all of our needs without investing a lot of time or money.

My area is a haven for garage sales. During the season, I check the local or neighborhood newspapers on Thursday and Friday and circle the ads indicating the items I need. Baby items, children's clothing, and toys are big sellers. It's the ultimate recycling effort! While it's fun to shop the up-scale neighborhoods, they aren't always the best places for children's bargains. The neighborhoods with lots of children are the best. As children grow, they outgrow clothes and get tired of toys. It's a real blessing to find a gently used, large plastic toy for a fraction of the store price, or a once-worn and outgrown party dress for a few dollars. Plan to arrive ten minutes before the stated sale time and happy hunting!

Another bargain source is thrift or consignment shops. Generally the prices are higher than garage or clothing sales, but these stores are good sources for dressy clothes at a fraction of the original cost. If your first visit is discouraging, keep coming back because the inventory always changes.

Clothing Sales and Exchanges

I was shocked to see the block-long line of women waiting at the first clothing sale I visited. And the excited women waiting to be allowed into the large hall to shop all held plastic bags and laundry baskets. Now I know why they were so excited!

Several groups in my area hold these sales twice a year. Look for them in your local newspapers. Typical sponsors might be a Juniors Club, Mothers of Twins, or church groups. If you have items to sell, you will receive a percentage of the sale price, and the remainder will go to the sponsoring organization. This is a major fund-raiser for some groups. For moms, it's a delight. I usually spend more than I make selling our items, but these sales make a substantial dent in our seasonal clothing budget.

Also, some churches offer clothing exchanges for their members. No money changes hands. Rather, the participants bring in their own items and are entitled to choose an equal number of items that suit their needs. No one has to do any bookkeeping, and the church and participants perform a substantial service for their member parents. If you don't have one at your church, maybe *you* should be the one to organize next season's exchange.

I do buy some new items, like socks, shoes, and underwear. But our kids don't mind used clothing. In fact when someone asks Clare where we got something, she proudly announces, "At a garage sale," even if the person is inquiring about our car or her sister.

I feel very strongly that the wise use of our resources will allow me to stay home longer with our children by delaying my return to work and is just good stewardship of our many blessings.

Preparing Clothes for Sales and Exchanges

If you want to preserve your clothes or prepare them for a clothing sale, here is a great stain removal recipe that I first came across on a registration form for a children's clothing sale. I have seen it so many times since that I think it has become part of modern mothering folklore.

In one gallon of hot water, mix one cup of automatic dishwasher detergent and a quarter cup of all-fabric bleach. Mix it thoroughly. Soak just a few items at a time for at least a few hours, preferably overnight. Rinse completely, then wash as usual. This hasn't worked on everything, but I have been very pleased with the results, even on old stains.

For white clothing, spray Tilex on the stain then wash immediately. This may bleach out colors if you use it on something other than whites, so be very careful.

Cleaning: Why Is My House Always a Mess?

Cleaning is always a matter of priorities. Some things must be done—you can't leave spilled food on the floor, but you can ignore dust if you have something better to do. But the only way to do intense cleaning at my house is to send the children away. Because this isn't practical, my house is rarely intensely cleaned. However, those who know me will forgive my messy house. They know we have better things to do.

Barbara Trudel says, "I sometimes have my husband take the kids out somewhere in the evening so I can have an hour or so to just give the house a once over without interruption. For the most part though, I really try to just take a deep breath and ask myself which is more important, the kids or the white glove test?"

Deniece Schofield, in her *Confessions of an Organized Housewife,* says you must first decide how much time you can or want to spend cleaning. How many days do you want to do heavy cleaning and how many days can you just maintain the chaos? Then she says to, "One by one, go through every room in your house. On a sheet of paper list everything you think needs to be done to thoroughly clean that room. Remember, this is according to you! How clean do you think the rooms need to be?" Finally, decide how often the work needs to be done—daily, weekly, monthly, or seasonally, keeping in mind that your "schedule needs to reflect your lifestyle and physical surroundings."[8]

Rene Jurkowski has a loose system that works well for her. "I have a schedule of a few household chores that get done on certain days of the week. So, if I have one of those rough days when nothing gets done, I can at least say to myself, 'I did the dusting today!' It's also much nicer than cleaning the whole house on one day." Another quick tip comes from Neleen Lehman, mother of five. She keeps a full set of cleaning supplies on each floor of her house to avoid running up and down to get them.

Nancy V., mother of two, says, "I used to be fairly regular about cleaning my house. Then Joseph turned two. His sense of order means that toys must be strewn throughout the house, that windows need a few streaks, and that every floor must have at least a few food crumbs on it. So now I try to remember that this is *his* house too, and I pick up as needed, usually while he's asleep."

Author Christine Davidson quips that, "My shocking deficiencies as a housekeeper saved us money—the less I vacuumed the house, the more electricity we saved. The more I served carrot and celery sticks for the vegetable at dinner instead of chopping and cooking them, the more gas we saved."[9] Mrs. Davidson also developed a household chore method that she dubbed "the incidental system of housework." Essentially, she does chores while she is doing something else—laundry while playing with the kids or washing dishes while helping with homework. In her philosophy, "the chores are incidental to what's really important in my life."[10]

Rene Jurkowski says, "In a hurry because unexpected company is coming over? Do a quick bathroom cleaning using a baby wipe. Run it over the toilet, sink, and faucets." Then you're ready for visitors. In fact, visitors are a good way to keep yourself somewhat disciplined. Lori Solyom says, "Have company often, even just a friend over for coffee every week or so. It will inspire, maybe force, you to keep your home presentable."

You can make cleaning a family affair and keep your husband involved, too. Jodi Benware, who is pregnant with her third child, cleans once a week with her husband. "We can get it all done in about half an hour," she says. As children get older, they can learn to actually help around the house. I taught our three- and four-year-olds a method to remember the chores they need to do in the morning. I drew a hand on a piece of paper and wrote the following on the five fingers: eat breakfast, brush teeth and wash, get dressed, pick up rooms, and watch TV or play. Instead of nagging, "Did you brush your teeth, or wash, or get dressed?" I can merely say, "Did you do all the fingers?" Plus, all the fingers need to be completed before play or TV. A great, built-in morning incentive is when the big purple dinosaur is on TV shortly after breakfast!

A great perspective on cleaning is expressed by Cindy McCabe, a mom at home. She says, "Within a month of staying home, I realized housework could consume all my time and energy. I vividly remember staring down a dust bunny and deciding I was staying home to raise my daughter and not to be a maid. Millions of people live in third world countries and survive quite well. I am trying to lose my perfectionist attitude toward a clean house." Ruth Gibson, who raised her kids in the sixties, says there was no pressure from anybody about anything when she was home with her kids. She keeps it all in perspective by reminding us, "Be thankful you have a house or apartment to clean! Get rid of clutter!"

What do you enjoy least about being home?

The lack of free time—my list of things to do often goes with only one or two things checked off.
—*Debbie Heinze*

Getting Help

Only one woman I spoke to in preparation for this book said one of her sacrifices to stay home with her children was to do without household help. But under some circumstances, household help is a necessity (like sickness of the mother or multiple births). Can you get it done at a respectable wage and stay within your budget?

Many high school and college students are anxious to earn some extra cash. Call your local schools and try to do some recruiting. My sister has a high school boy (a friend's son) come to do chores that are more than she wants to handle, like shampooing rugs or painting the bathroom. He enjoys conversation with an adult other than his mom, and my sister gets some work done at an affordable wage.

Just as the women mentioned earlier had a cooking co-op, perhaps you can organize a chore co-op with friends or neighbors. Is there a job you detest that you would be willing to trade some baby-sitting or other chore to have a neighbor handle for you? For example, another sister of mine *hated* cleaning the oven. Her girlfriend didn't mind, so my sister would cook for her and entertain her while she came over to clean the oven. They ended up making a delightful evening of fun and fellowship out of a nasty job. With a little creativity and brainstorming with your good friends and neighbors, you may think of some other swaps that would benefit everyone, like trading haircuts for chores or yard work for baby-sitting.

11

Finances

Budget. Just mentioning the word makes me want to change the subject. Let's talk about something else. Let's talk about root canal surgery. Anything but budgets. But they're a fact of life. I finally got over the negative image of budgets by thinking of them as financial plans. The day-to-day decisions we make about our money are shaping our finances for the future. Denise Wickline, a mom at home, says this about budgets: "They're freeing, not oppressive." They can be necessary guides and boundaries for our lives and lifestyles.

Yours versus His Is Now Ours

Like many formerly employed mothers, I lamented the loss of my income. I had earned my own money since the age of thirteen. For me, my salary equaled my independence. As long as I was earning my own money, I didn't need anyone else. I could take care of myself. Whenever I think of this early attitude, I am reminded of a pouting little girl who, when disappointed, responds by saying, "I don't need you anyway!" Given my life history, I didn't trust God or my husband to provide for my needs. I felt I had to grit my teeth, put my shoulder to the wheel, and take care of everything myself.

But somewhere along the line, I realized that God was never going to let me down. "Great is your faithfulness," became my life verse (Lam. 3:23). As I looked back over my life, I realized that God had always been there looking out for me, carrying me when I couldn't walk alone, and providing for all my needs when the world disappointed me. When I began to really feel that trust, I began to trust my husband and other people as well. They are the blessings God has sent to me to tell me of his faithfulness. Who am I to doubt?

Husbands and wives have to reach a balance on the issue of money. There may have to be new rules. There may even have to be a new vocabulary to keep the subject less emotionally charged. Like instead of *his* money and *her* money, it becomes *our* money. Marnie Murray says, "I never felt it was *his* money. We are a team. Everything is *ours*." A sensitive husband even acknowledges that his wife's work at home benefits him. Perri Haughwout says that her husband "considers the money from his salary as 'our' salary, and he lets me know that he wouldn't be as successful as he is without my support."

Many women reported feeling guilty for not earning a salary, but there are many reasons *not* to feel guilty. Norma Kunda, a Ph.D. mom at home, reminds us that, "My services to my family are worth a great deal." Barbara Trudel put it this way: "I finally realized that I didn't need to be a financial equal in order to be an equal partner in my marriage." Rene Jurkowski has worked out a system with her husband that eliminates some of the "his versus mine" issue. She says, "We each have some personal fun money built into our monthly budget that we can spend on whatever we want—no questions asked."

What is your perspective on money? How do you feel about it? Is it a power issue in your marriage? Does it cause you to feel insecure? When you and your husband are dealing with the nuts and bolts of a new budget, you each need to be able to keep your emotions under control and try to examine the facts objectively.

Cheryl Ammons, a young but very wise mother at home has a helpful perspective. She says, "We consider all of our money as the Lord's and we are the stewards of his money. We aim to bring him glory through our finances." With this attitude, she and her husband "watch as God supernaturally works to meet our needs."

There will come a time when you will earn money again. Until then, it may be helpful to look at your role a little differently.

Managing and Saving Money—Your New Role

Marnie Murray says, "My financial role in our family has changed from revenue producer to investment manager and cost container." In other words, you can view the money you save as your financial contribution to the family, just as your salary was your contribution before. As a mother at home, your role now can be to pour your effort into learning new and creative ways to economize and lower costs.

I believe God wants us to be good stewards of his gifts, and part of that good stewardship is a budget. (Oh no—there's that word again!) Proverbs 27:23 has often been interpreted as the biblical admonition to keep a budget: "Be sure you know the condition of your flocks, give careful attention to your herds." Just as this passage talks about the importance of "budgeting" livestock, I believe God wants us to know where we stand financially. In other words, is your budget in order?

Many of us need a new mind-set about the issue of budgeting. Less is more, in many respects. And remember that your commitment to mothering full-time places people over possessions. When talking about finances and possessions in *Margin*, Dr. Richard Swensen says, "God comes first and possessions come second. . . . Possessions are to be used not loved. . . . Tragically, for many Americans today, their empty lives do indeed consist in the abundance of their possessions."[1] Focusing attention on the abundance in the other aspects of our lives, while learning to live with less, can be liberating! But to keep people first and possessions second, you have to control your possessions rather than allowing them to control you.

Taking a good, hard, and accurate look at your financial picture is the first step toward getting a handle on your money and spending habits. When it's all in black and white, it is easier to see what areas need work. What are your assets and your liabilities? Writing these down is called creating a balance sheet, which is pretty simple to do. On one piece of paper, make a list of everything you own and what it is worth. On another piece, make a list of everything you *owe*. When you compare the totals of what you own (assets) and what you owe (liabilities or debts), you will have a clear picture of your financial health.

If you are heavily in debt, look at the character of that debt. A mortgage with payments you can comfortably afford is one thing. Lots of credit cards or short-term loans is another. If you have many assets, examine them to determine if they are working hard enough for you. You may want to consult a trusted broker or financial planner.

If you have many more debts than assets, you have some work to do. You can deal with this situation by either increasing your income to keep up with your debts, or learning to cut back on spending. Making a budget will help show you, in black and white, where to cut back. It is amazing to me that an (overly) educated person like myself resisted this process for so long. I put it off for *years*. I shudder to think of how much farther ahead we might be if we had planned better from the beginning of our marriage.

To make a budget, you have to keep track of everything you spend for a few months. I carry a small notebook and jot down every expenditure. At the end of a week or two, I transfer those amounts to a budget sheet, like the one in chapter 3 of this book. Then I fill in the rest of the budget sheet with the other monthly expenses to see where all the money goes each month.

If your expenses are not payable monthly, you need to break them down to a monthly amount so you know how much to set aside each month for that category. For example, if you spend eight hundred dollars per year on children's clothing, you need to allocate about sixty-seven dollars per month to cover that expense. If your car breaks down a couple of times a year at a cost of five hundred dollars per incident, take one thousand dollars, divide it by twelve, and set aside eighty-four dollars per month for automobile repairs.

The two excuses I used most often to avoid a budget were unplanned expenses and fluctuations in income. But if you think about it, few expenses are really unplanned. For example, if you look over what you spent on medical bills last year, you can probably figure that the kids are going to get at least that number of ear infections again this year. Figure out that cost on a monthly basis, and you will know how much to set aside. The same goes for car repairs or for appliances that probably need to be replaced in the near future.

Fluctuations in my income from legal fees was not a valid excuse to avoid budgeting either. Many people are in this situation, including salesmen whose earnings fluctuate through the year. However, you can still get an accurate monthly picture by examining your yearly income from your tax forms for the last several years. An average of those amounts will be an accurate predictor of where you will stand in the current year.

To help you organize and maintain your budget, many fine budget workbooks are available. You can buy one from a book or stationery store or create your own for pennies. A book you make yourself will be personalized to your unique family situation, including categories for karate lessons or cat supplies. Once you have an idea of where it all goes, you can begin to plug the leaks in your financial boat.

As you examine your situation and consider certain sacrifices, remember that "Faith grows well in a financial climate that forces us to trust God instead of our own ability to earn a living."[2] Engrave the following verse over the place where you and your husband have your money discussions and let it guide you through this adventure: "Trust in the Lord with all your heart and lean not on your own understanding; in all your ways acknowledge him, and he will make your paths straight" (Prov. 3:5–6). If it is the deep desire of your heart to have a season at home, pour out your heart to the Lord and ask him to guide you to ways that will make it possible.

Savings and Daily Money Management

The advice is old, but true. You have to pay yourself first. Whatever amount you decide to save, make sure it is the *first* amount allocated out of each pay period. We find it easier to have our savings removed before we actually see the paycheck. Like Barbara Trudel says, "We do a good job saving money by having it deducted from my husband's pay and sent immediately to various savings accounts and mutual funds." In our family, we then track those accounts and funds each month to make sure the proper amounts were credited and to check the performance of the investments. And because this is money that we never actually *see*, we don't miss it.

Are you susceptible to impulse spending? Cut up your credit cards or put them in your safe deposit box. Leave your checkbook and your automated teller machine (ATM) card at home. (Our children now believe that *all* machines give money because they have seen me use the ATM so often!) If you're really serious about saving money, try giving yourself an allotted amount of cash for the week. When it's gone, you simply can't spend anymore. You may find (as I did) that you did much of your spending simply because money was available.

Make sure you have free checking. If you have to maintain a balance to avoid service charges, do it. Our bank offers free checking with the direct deposit of my husband's paychecks. We highly recommend direct deposit, and as an added benefit, you may not have to pay for checking.

Take an inventory of all the items in your wallet. Write down all the account numbers as well as the phone numbers to call if they are lost. If you lose your wallet, you may not remember to cancel your video or library card. With an inventory on hand, you will be ready to make all the necessary phone calls.

Caron LaPlante says, "I save all our change and roll it up a few times a year and save it. That comes to two hundred dollars to three hundred dollars a year." Small change, but it could amount to a deposit on a vacation cabin, or a new dryer that must be purchased in an emergency. We also make a big deal out of our children's piggy banks. A couple of times a year, we empty them out and carry the coins to the bank together so they can see them counted and deposited in their individual savings accounts.

Your Home

When author Marilee Horton quit her job to come home to raise her children, she heard her pastor teach a lesson on Philippians 4:19—"And my God will meet all your needs according to his glorious riches in Christ Jesus." She was impressed by the fact that God promised to supply "needs, not wants."[3]

What do you really need in a home? Prior generations were more willing to make do with worn carpeting and an old sofa. Many young families seem to think that their house has to be perfect, even early in a marriage when small children are entering the family. They pay a high price for this material choice. Two jobs are needed to make the furniture payment, the van payment, and the pool payment as well as everything else. Is all this really that important to you? A simpler lifestyle means less stress and more time for your family to spend together. They will remember the afternoons spent making macaroni necklaces. They won't remember that the table was worn and the chairs were rickety. As Ruth Gibson says, she was always "thankful that she had a home to clean."

Is it time to consider refinancing your castle? As of this writing, interest rates are still low. If you are able to shave a few points of interest off your loan, it could result in substantial savings. In addition, if you have some equity built up in your home, you could use that equity to pay off some higher-rate debts. Ask your lender to show you the exact facts and figures for your situation. It costs you nothing to investigate.

Also, learn to do minor home repairs and redecorating yourself. There are many fine how-to books in the library to teach you or your husband to fix a leaky faucet or replace a frayed wire. My husband has saved us a fortune by learning to do some home maintenance that he had no desire to learn, but graciously handled because it was more economical. (He can now rod out the drains, and saves us an incredible amount on plumbing bills.) We repainted the entire interior of our house ourselves, one room at a time, and replaced some trim. Although it was sometimes a hassle, I look around my little house with great pride because I know that those brush strokes and that plastering job were done by *us*.

Shopping, Shopping, Shopping

I love to shop. It is sometimes a struggle for me to forgo shopping with wild abandon as I did in the old days. Previously, we lived in an economically depressed area with few shopping options, but because we were both working professionals, we had a lot of expendable income. Then we moved to our present location, a shopper's paradise, but we cut down to one salary and have little, if any, discretionary money. God does indeed have a sense of humor!

Janice Smullen, a mom at home, says her best tips on saving money are to, "tithe, don't go to the mall, and refuse to go to buying parties." Good advice. But what are some day-to-day ways you can cut down that shopping bill for all of your household needs?

Many grocery stores have provided a built-in system to help us keep on a budget. It is called unit pricing. In most of the larger stores, there is a little placard on the shelf under each item. On that card is the price, the unit of measure, and the price per unit. For example, a sixteen-ounce can of vegetables sells for eighty-nine cents. On the same shelf, the generic version of the same product is a twelve-ounce can that sells for seventy-nine cents. Which is the better buy? The unit pricing on the placard will tell you, in this instance, that the brand name is actually a better price, at 5.56 cents per ounce, over the generic brand at 6.58 cents per ounce. Unit prices are calculated for almost every item in the store, from ounces of cereal to the number of paper towels per roll. It pays to check. When using a coupon, whip out your calculator, subtract the coupon amount from the price, then calculate the unit price. Are you really saving? The information is there for us to use.

Another way to save is by getting information from an under-utilized resource offered by the United States Government called the Consumer Information Center. They have a little catalog with hundreds of mostly free government publications on consumer issues. You can request a free catalog by writing to this address:

Consumer Information Center
Pueblo, CO 81009

Gardening and Farmers Markets

Can you productively use space in your yard to plant a garden? This is not only a fun way to share nature with your children, but it can also save you money on vegetables at the market. And you can pick up canning jars and supplies from garage sales for a few pennies, so your family can have healthy, inexpensive foods from your garden all year round. Look out in your yard and ask yourself if you are making the most productive use of that space. Be sure to save space for yard play and mud pies, of course. If gardening, canning, or drying food is all new to you, your local Co-operative Extension Service can be a great source of free or inexpensive informational materials. Look in the "County" section of your phone book to find out if there is one in your area.

As an alternative, many urban areas offer farmers markets in the summer. These are a wonderful source of fresh produce that is often priced less than the supermarket. Also, if you want to can some foods you have not grown yourself, you may often purchase them in bulk from one of these markets. Contact your city or village hall to find out if these markets are held in your area.

Coupons and Rebates

Are coupons worth the hassle? Remember that the manufacturer's motivation is to get you to try a new product. Make sure you compare the cost of the product after deducting the coupon with the cost of your usual brand by checking the unit price as described above. But the wisest use of coupons is to buy products you use all the time, like your usual detergent.

In an entire book on couponing, author Susan Samtur suggests the best use of coupons and gives suggestions for organization. You may purchase a copy by calling the following number:

> Susan Samtur
> The Super Coupon Shopping System
> Hyperion Press
> 1-800-759-0190

Rebating is another way to save on your purchases. A refund or rebate is an amount of money manufacturers will send when you send them proof of the purchase of a product. They usually require three things: a rebate form obtained from the store, a UPC code from the product, and your sales register receipt showing the purchase. In exchange for assembling these items, a manufacturer will send you a small check or some other item.

Many women claim to supplement their family income and also obtain free products by sending in rebates. If you want to learn more about rebating, write to these specialized newsletters for subscription information:

> *Money Talk*
> P. O. Box 1677
> Kingston, PA 18704

> *Refunding Makes Sense*
> P. O. Box R
> Farmington, UT 84025

> *Refund World*
> P. O. Box 16001W
> Philadelphia, PA 19114

Miscellaneous Money-Stretching Tips

Remember when you're shopping for groceries that convenience has a cost. Denise Wickline says, "By avoiding refined convenience foods, we save money in the long run as well as time—fewer illnesses, doctor visits, and time lost to healing. We eat food that's simple and as close to its natural form as possible." Denise is a wonderful example of a mom who is a careful steward of God's gifts.

Diluting can also make products last longer. Our kids usually drink sugar-free juice, and lots of it! We often dilute this to stretch it a bit. You can also dilute cleaning products and shampoo. Most are too strong anyway, especially shampoo.

Many women make their own soft soap for their pump dispensers. Cover leftover soap chips with boiling water and when they're melted, pour the mix into the pump container.

Another popular item to make at home is baby wipes. Rene Jurkowski makes her own with paper towels, baby bath soap, and baby oil. These can be stored in a zipper plastic bag or other plastic container, and they work just as well as more expensive ones from the store.

Do you know what products are lurking in your cabinets? Clean out your cupboards and think of creative, tasty dishes to make with that canned asparagus and those garbanzo beans before they are too old to use. Take an inventory of how many cans of tomato sauce you have so you don't keep buying more. Are there half-used containers of cleaners you forgot you had? It's silly to have this stuff taking up space if you're not going to use it.

Automobiles

Do you need two cars? Could you make do with one by driving your husband to work or to the train a few days a week so you can have the car for errands? The savings here can be tremendous. You will save on automobile insurance, gasoline, car payments, tires, repairs, and maintenance. We have been a single-car family for two years, and there have only been a few times we have missed the luxury of two cars. Also, don't forget to use public transportation if it is available to you. I am always amazed when I drive to downtown Chicago and see so many people sitting by themselves on the expressway in their cars in unbearable traffic every day. You or your husband can save a tremendous amount of money by commuting rather than driving.

When purchasing a car, it makes better financial sense to look for a good used car rather than a new one. Consider this fact—car dealers estimate that a new vehicle loses two thousand dollars in value the minute you drive it off the dealer lot, because it is no longer a new car. Are you really willing to pay that much just for that new car smell? A wise purchase of a used car, perhaps one examined by a trusted mechanic friend, is a much better financial deal than buying new.

Also, if you do have an older car, it doesn't make sense to keep full insurance coverage on it. Liability insurance is all that is required in most states. The really expensive coverage is the collision or comprehensive coverage. If your car is older, it might be worth it to carry just the minimum insurance.

Speaking of insurance, do you know your deductible? The deductible is the amount you pay out of pocket before the insurance company kicks in their coverage. The higher the deductible, the lower the insurance premium. Check your policy. If your deductible is one hundred dollars, call your agent and ask what you could save by raising it to five hundred dollars or even one thousand dollars.

Kid Stuff

Do your children have a bad case of the gimmies? We find that if the kids keep the dial tuned to public television, they are less likely to beg for the latest doo-dad. We try to limit their viewing of commercial television to a minimum, which really helps to keep their requests down.

Another place to save is on sitters. You can save a lot on sitters by forming or joining a baby-sitting co-op. One of my mom's groups has one, and the system is quite simple. Each participating mom is issued a number of index cards with half an hour, one hour, or two hours designated on the card. She then uses the cards to "pay" the sitting mom for the amount of time she uses. Conversely, when she watches another child, she is "paid" the appropriate number of cards. No money changes hands, and the system can be a lifesaver for all the moms involved. Check with your local women's groups or parent support organizations to see if a baby-sitting co-op already exists. If not, put up some notices in your neighborhood and get one started.

How many invitations for children's birthday parties do you get each year? It's staggering. And the money parents spend for parties is amazing. In my area, some parents almost seem to try to out-do one another. And merchants are only too happy to assist. Play arenas and restaurants will host your child's party for a price. But we prefer to keep our parties simple, if we invite guests at all. Our daughters make gifts and cards for one another, and we always look for ideas for inexpensive presents. We are reexamining whether it is really necessary to invite fifteen preschoolers to our home for a party. Not only is it a headache, but we also can expect to have to shell out gifts for the fifteen preschooler parties we will be invited to attend over the following year. It doesn't make sense, and we are consciously trying to tame the birthday/holiday monster. There are wonderful ways to make your child feel special besides having an elaborate party.

Look for clothing, sporting goods, and toy swaps or exchanges in your area. You can save a fortune on soccer uniforms or ballet slippers by buying what Joey or Janey down the block outgrew last season.

> ## What do you enjoy most about being home?
>
> *I enjoy knowing that I am influencing my own children. They are learning our family values, and I can truly see and know their hearts at every stage. I love helping them learn.*
> —Laura Englehart

Also, make your own Halloween costumes. When I was growing up in the '60s and '70s with my seven brothers and sisters, we would always dress as hobos for Halloween. With some raggedy clothes and some charcoal to make our faces dirty, we were all set. But for our children, it is more complicated. They are brainwashed into thinking that they have to emulate the latest Disney heroine at Halloween. Encourage your children to keep this holiday simple and fun, if you even choose to celebrate it at all. Go for the playful, fun, dress-up ideas, like making butterfly wings or fashioning a bride dress out of an old sheet. The joy is in the creativity, not in merely imitating something they have seen on TV or at the movies.

Use scrap paper or junk mail for coloring. We go through reams of paper at my house. Any reasonably uncluttered surface is usable. Don't waste it! Also, learn to cut your children's hair (and possibly your husband's). There is a good how-to book called *How to Cut Children's Hair* by Bob Bent (New York: Simon & Schuster, 1977). It is available at most libraries. This could be fun outside with a garden hose, a wading pool, and some buckets of hot water.

Miscellaneous Tips

Get your financial records in order. Buy plastic boxes, a filing cabinet, or whatever organizational method suits your fancy. Get file folders, in different colors if that will help you get organized. Make lists of your accounts and assets. Chart how your investments are faring. With this written information at your fingertips, you will be in a better position to wisely manage your money.

When tax time comes around, remember that the IRS Publication 17, "Your Federal Income Tax," is free. It is a comprehensive guide to preparing your taxes. If you send for it early enough to make sure you get a copy, it could save you the cost of purchasing a tax preparation guide. On the subject of taxes, keep a record of all your cash charitable contributions, especially if most of your giving is in cash. You will want to give an accurate figure at the end of the year. Make a note of each contribution in your expenditure book.

If you love to read all the new books, keep in mind that your local library has an acquisitions budget. Is there a twenty-two dollar hardback book you've been wanting to read? Ask your librarian to order it. You may have to wait a bit to read the book, but you will save some cash.

We love to entertain, but trying to put on a big spread can be beyond our budget. Lori Solyom likes to save money by having friends over for a pot-luck dinner, or a dessert and coffee night. A party is a party, no matter how much money you've spent on it. You might actually be more relaxed and have more fun!

Barter is big news. Items such as office equipment or clothing as well as services can be traded. Some services include printing, secretarial service, photography, legal services, accounting, janitorial services, or catering. Whatever your skill, talent, or interest, chances are someone can use your help and can trade you something of value for it. A good basic book on bartering and how to set up your own trade club is called *The Barter Way to Beat Inflation* by George Burtt (New York: Everest House, 1980), available at most libraries. If your area has a trade group established, it would be listed in the phone book under "Barter" or "Trading Clubs." However, most bartering is done on an informal basis between families and friends. One mom might do haircuts for a month in exchange for your husband tilling their garden. Be creative! Think about the resources and skills available just in your own neighborhood. The money you all can save by pooling and sharing those talents could be considerable.

Shop around for credit card interest rates. Companies vary widely in what they have to offer. Check the fine print for yearly fees and the method of calculating interest. Could you do better than you're doing? Many companies will allow you to transfer a balance which you can then whittle down at a lower interest rate.

Rent movies instead of going out. Have a family movie night with lots of popcorn and soft drinks. Invite another family to share the fun. Also, cancel cable subscriptions for channels you don't watch or need. Or cancel your service entirely and put your TV in storage for a while. Do you think you could live without it?

Cancel subscriptions to magazines or papers you don't read. What do you realistically get around to fully enjoying? You could also swap magazines with a friend, or check them out at your local library, saving you a great deal each year.

For summer family entertainment, many communities host free community concerts. A night under the stars on a blanket with a picnic dinner can be a special family memory, and the cost to you is nil.

Explore the resources your community has available for family entertainment and nature appreciation, and remember your frugality won't have to last forever. Be creative and enjoy it!

Part-Time Income Opportunities at Home

For many women, earning extra income while at home makes a season at home possible. Home day care is one of the most popular methods. "It makes you your own boss, eliminates leaving your baby, and eliminates the costs of transportation and clothing purchases for your job. And, you are not owned by anyone . . . child care is a family affair with everyone involved with some phase of entertainment or care giving," says author Mary Ann Cahill.[4] Our former day care provider had three children of her own. It was not unusual to see them giving a bottle or to see her husband fry up some bacon for breakfast.

> *What do you enjoy least about being home?*
>
> *I am sometimes very tired and would like to be "off duty" for a while.*
> —Jackie Wellwood

Before and after school care is also badly needed. And it is a chance to minister to our sisters who must work by providing them with reliable care for their children during the gaps in work/school schedules. A helping mother who is willing to make a special trip to take a working mom's child to a ballet class is a rare and special blessing, too.

Some other ideas that women in my survey came up with are below:

- Home bakery. Bake homemade bread to sell WARM to neighbors or small stores. Jackie Wellwood is making plans to do this in her neighborhood as a project to do with her daughters and to add a few dollars to their family budget.
- Personal shopper for people who are too busy to do their own shopping.

- Home sewing. This could include alterations, repairs, or making children's clothes.
- Phone sales, collections, or market research. Many companies are thrilled to find people to work a few hours a day from home.
- Newspaper delivery. One mom I knew delivered papers in the wee hours of the morning while her family slept. She incurred no baby-sitting expense and added nicely to her family income.
- Furniture upholstery and refinishing can be done in a roomy basement or garage.
- Portrait photography with a personal touch can be done by a mom who goes to another mom's house.
- Direct sales. Many women sell cosmetics or baskets and are able to work around their family schedules.
- Cleaning business. Offices can be cleaned at night and houses can be cleaned during the day with a little one in tow.
- Sell crafts at malls, fairs, or shops. At Christmas, Laura Englehart sold painted shirts. Susan Fenton runs a handmade stationery business out of her home.
- Tutoring or lessons. Many former teachers or musicians do home tutoring or music lessons.
- School crossing guard. These women work with their children's schedule. Inquire at your local police department about these jobs.
- Office work, bookkeeping, computer work, writing, or editing. These jobs are a natural for the home worker.
- Flower arranging. Do you love baskets and silk flowers? Maybe you can turn this interest into a profitable sideline.
- Custom gift baskets. Many people are too busy to shop for that special gift. A custom basket can incorporate some of the interests of the receiver, such as coffee, crafts, or candy.

- House sitting or apartment management.
- Party planning. You can plan children's parties or weddings. Having someone to take care of the details can be very valuable to a busy family.
- Pet sitting or plant care. You can serve individual clients or do plant care for offices.
- Résumé writing. If you have a computer with a good printer and a flair for writing, you can help students and others put together résumés.
- Ironing or laundry. Put an ad in your local newspaper or hang notices at the laundromat.
- Nail and hair care. Sally Murrow, a mom at home, also has a hair salon at home.
- Cake decorating or catering. If your gift is cooking, you can start one of these businesses in your kitchen.
- Tax preparation. Donna Pindel, mom, attorney, and CPA, earns occasional income by preparing tax returns and doing real estate closings.

The following are some sources for information about at-home businesses:

Mothers Home Business Network, P. O. Box 423, East Meadow, NY 11554.

The Work-at-Home Sourcebook: How to Find At-Home Work That's Right for You by Lynie Arden (Boulder: Live Oak Publications, 1987). This book lists actual employers who use home workers.

The Best Home Businesses for the '90s by Paul and Sarah Edwards (Los Angeles: Jeremy P. Tarcher, Inc., 1991). This book lists many creative ideas with practical information on how to get started and how to find clients.

Internal Revenue Service Publication 587, "Business Use of Your Home."

An Interview with a Child Care Provider

Karen Dawson is the mother of two children, ages three and eight. During the school year, she provides full-time care for an infant and after-school care for grade school children. Also, check in Karen's backyard on a summer afternoon, and you are likely to see many of the neighborhood children on her swing set or playing in the grass. Her home is warm and inviting, and she instantly makes visitors feel at home.

How long have you cared for children in your home?

"On and off for eight years, since my first child was born. It was really great to watch another child who was my daughter's age. She had a built-in playmate and loved it."

How do parents locate you?

"Word of mouth and by referral."

Don't you get tired?

"Yes, but no more tired than I do caring for my own children. I feel it's almost my ministry—that I can be here for kids whose moms have to work. I can give them some sense of security."

How important is it for you to stay home with your own children?

"I want to give them security and let them know they can count on me. I want them to remember a stable home where I was available for them."

Why don't you take in more children?

"I don't think I could give them all the attention they needed. Also, I'm not set up at my house to care for more children."

Why do the neighborhood kids like to visit you so much?

"I like to let the kids play freely and enjoy themselves. Also, I like to play *with them*, and we all enjoy!"

An Interview with a Home Small Business Worker

Susan Fenton is the mother of two children, ages five and eighteen months. She has a homemade stationery business that she operates out of her home. The product is sold at craft displays and through mail order.

How did you get the idea for this business?

"It started with my husband and me doing our own Christmas cards, and it went from there. I learned embossing and some other skills, and people started to place orders with me."

How much time do you spend in an average week?

"About eight to ten hours. During the holiday season when I have a lot of gift orders, it may expand to twenty hours."

Where do you work?

"On my dining room table. I'm less efficient because I have to take everything out and put everything away each time I work."

Where would you like to see your business go?

"I'd like to spend twenty-five to thirty hours a week at it, building up a mail order business, and incorporate my kids into working, as I plan to home school them."

How will your children help?

"They are already interested! My five-year-old makes his own stationary. I'd like to use the business as a teaching tool for math skills and art. Also, if the kids are a part of the business, they won't feel like it infringes on our time as a family."

How important is it for you to stay home with your own children?

"It is very important. We are their primary influences. I want to be there to enjoy their moment-by-moment development."

What do you like best about working at home?

"It is a very satisfying creative outlet. The repetitiveness of chores at home is balanced by my making something beautiful. This balance is important to me and to my family."

12

Taking Care of Ourselves

Do you feel guilty when you take time for yourself? Taking care of and nurturing yourself is one way to love yourself. The Bible tells us in Matthew 22:37–39 to love the Lord, love your neighbor, and love *yourself.* As mothers, sometimes we are so engaged in loving and caring for our families that we forget to care for ourselves. This tendency to put our needs last leaves us vulnerable to becoming out of balance. Taken to the extreme, Denise Wickline says, "It's senseless to feel that it is somehow noble to drive yourself to despair." While we do have enormous responsibilities at home, we are also responsible for nurturing ourselves before we reach mommy burnout.

Balancing Four Dimensions

Emilie Barnes, author of *Things Happen When Women Care*, reminds us that we all need to refresh and renew ourselves in four dimensions of our nature. They are our spiritual selves, our physical selves, our mental selves, and our emotional selves. She tells the story of a man trying to cut down a tree with a dull saw. It took forever because he did not take the time to sharpen the saw.[1] The Bible says, "A dull axe requires great strength; be wise and sharpen the blade" (Eccles. 10:10 TLB). Renewing ourselves is a way of sharpening our saws so we will be more effective in all aspects of our lives. Barbara Trudel says, "Just as my husband takes periodic business trips to seminars and workshops in order to be a better doctor, I need time away from my kids to renew myself in order to be a better mom."

It comes down to balance. You need to balance all the responsibilities and joys of your life and still take care of yourself. If you ignore that balance for any significant period of time, you run the risk of burnout, which has consequences for your health, emotions, and spirit.

For me, burnout is the feeling I have when I realize that I am living my life without living my day. I am so rushed or preoccupied that I haven't stopped to catch the joy of that day. It is the feeling that Job had when he said, "My days are swifter than a weaver's shuttle" (Job 7:6). If this hurryness goes on for a long period of time, I get physically sick. A case of bronchitis always reminds me that I have been pushing too hard and that I need to just let the river flow. When I am fortunate enough to catch my balance before actually becoming ill, I am grateful. I can then turn to my Source, my God, who orders my days and restores my soul. A solid relationship with him is the only real remedy for burnout. If we put that relationship first as a preventative, our lives will have a measure of balance.

The Spiritual Dimension

An oddity of life for me is that the busier I am, the more time I need to spend in prayer with my God. When that time gets set aside due to a busy schedule, everything seems out of whack. The busier I am, the more I need to pray to discern if my busyness is what God is truly willing for my life.

When his life was crowding around Jesus and he needed to get away, he invited the apostles to "Come with me by yourselves to a quiet place and get some rest" (Mark 6:31). Every day, he offers the same invitation to us—to come away to have fellowship with him and rest in his arms. He longs for our fellowship. He wants us to rest from our busyness and know the joy of a relationship with him.

Sometimes I come away from this rest convinced that I need to slow things down to restore balance and sanity. Other times I come away with added inner strength, peace, and determination to see a busy time through to completion. Either way, the pace of my life does not make sense unless I cast my concerns on my God. His guidance in these times often helps me to avoid feeling frustrated.

Have you heard people say, "I'm too busy to pray or read the Bible"? Author Donna Otto says, "There is always time in your day to do the things your heart desires. Every day holds minutes or hours for prayer, Bible study, and reflection."[2] Ms. Otto suggests making a modest commitment of even five to eight minutes a day for Bible study. Keeping a Bible handy in each room of the house makes this easier. Ask God to make time with him a deep desire of your heart, and you will find a way. Even a short period of time, if approached diligently and prayerfully, can help you maintain spiritual balance.

Lori Solyom relies on bubbles, Bible, and books. She says, "About three times a week I insist on a bubble bath while Daddy is in charge of the children. I need that time to relax and read." She relies on cups of tea and Bible and prayer time out of the bathtub as well, when her three young daughters cooperate.

I can remember when I was trying to balance career and children that prayer was not often a part of my day. If it had been, maybe I would have handled it better. But one of the many blessings I have received since coming home to raise our children has been a spiritual renewal. There was little space for God in my hectic life before. Now I have made him the ruler of my days and have carved out time to thank and worship him daily. The benefit of slowing down the pace of my life to be with God has been a renewed relationship with him.

Does your church have a women's Bible study? Many churches not only offer topics of interest to women but also provide child care, a necessity for harried moms. The discipline, fellowship, and inspiration of a weekly Bible study with other Christian women can make your life at home much smoother.

Here are several other things you can do on your own to help you keep your spiritual equilibrium:

- Browse at a Christian bookstore for devotional materials. There are many fine daily prayer books and Bible study guides available. Find one that looks interesting and commit just ten minutes a day to refreshing your spirit with the Word of God.

- Write your prayers down in a journal. You can keep a small notebook in your purse or even write them at the computer. It is a great joy to read these over at a later date and note the many answers to prayer you have received.

- Write a prayer for your children. Ask God to build them into godly young men and women. Write down your desires for your children as a legacy for them, and review what you have written often.

- Get the program schedule for your local Christian radio station and let your mind bathe in beautiful Christian music during the day. There are Bible study programs on the radio as well. Even if your hands are busy tending to children, you can spend some time each day listening and praying.

Donna Otto reminds us to turn to the Source of our strength. She says, "You will never possess enough human love to stay at home, sacrifice for your children, and raise them the way God directs. . . . It is God's love that gives you the grace that is sufficient to every challenge of mothering."[3] When you are approaching a phase of mother burnout, remember that God's love, through the Holy Spirit, can rekindle the flame of your passion to be the best mother he wants you to be. Ask God daily for wisdom and strength in your job of mothering, and he will never fail you.

---

*W*hat do you enjoy most about being home?

I get to see the many, many special qualities in my children.

—*Jackie Wellwood*

The Physical Dimension

I love to overcomplicate things. I love to read, think, and plan, but I sometimes fall short in putting things into action. Maintaining physical balance means tending to the simple things—eat well, exercise a little, drink a lot of water, and get enough sleep. You can read a lot of books about these things, buy tapes, and attend special classes, or you can *just do* them. I generally err on the side of thinking about health and fitness too much rather than working at it. So one of my current prayers is asking God to guide me to physical health and help me develop a healthy mind-set. I ask him to guide me to proper foods and activities to maintain and improve my health.

Your health will also benefit if you learn to relax. A time set aside in prayer can actually help you to relax and to keep your physical self in balance. The greatest teacher, Jesus, maintained balance this way. The Bible says, "But Jesus often withdrew to lonely places and prayed" (Luke 5:16). When the pressures grew and demands from people increased, he took time to refresh, renew, and wait upon God for guidance. Even if we can't physically slip away to a retreat, exercise is also a great time to pray *and* tend to our physical and spiritual selves.

The Mental Dimension

I *love* being a mother, but I regularly need a diversion from motherhood. On a day when our children have been extremely emotionally draining, I sometimes feel my brain turning to mush. While mothering requires enormous creativity and patience, we need to exercise other skills to challenge our minds and keep them sharp. Here are some ways I have found to keep the mental saw sharpened:

- Read newspapers or news magazines to keep up on world issues. Try to read the editorials and commentaries to find out what people are debating.
- Read a lot! I aspire to read more literature, but don't seem to get to it. Does your local library have a Great Books discussion group? Get some books for yourself as well as the kids when you go to the library.
- Write a journal of poems, prayers, and thoughts. This can actually help you maneuver through a difficult time and do some problem-solving on paper.
- Rejuvenate the lost art of letter writing. When was the last time you sat down to write a really good letter to a friend or relative? These letters are a joy to receive and can be a good mental exercise to compose.

- Take a class. Opportunities for adult education are everywhere. Check with your high school, junior college, and park district.
- Discover a hobby. Have you secretly longed to learn to make pottery? Take a class. Ask a friend to teach you the basics of cross stitch. These pursuits can be rewarding and relaxing.
- Learn to play a musical instrument, or sharpen your skills on one you already play. You'll not only satisfy your creative urge, but you'll also set a great example for the kids.

The Emotional Dimension

A simple change in attitude can change everything. Remember the old commercial about the woman at the sewing machine whose children kept interrupting? She yelled at them and felt guilty afterwards. Could she have taken that moment to make a memory with her kids instead? A simple change in mom's attitude can set the mood for the house for the whole day. Take a deep breath. Think before you react. If you are the emotional barometer of your family, make sure you do all you can to keep the barometric pressure under control. When the kids are having a wild day, your calmness and peacefulness can help tame their craziness.

Laugh a lot. Our children regularly get the giggles. Instead of just acknowledging their humor, I join them. We might giggle together for ten minutes. When we're done, we're closer, and we have shared something special.

Also, good friends can help you keep your emotional balance. Develop friendships and take the time to nurture them. If you are feeling sorry for yourself because no one calls you for lunch, make a phone call and take the initiative to set the lunch date.

And express gratitude to God and to others for the blessings in your life. Our pastor tells the old story about Satan and his barn full of the seeds of discontent. The only place they won't grow is in a grateful heart. If you give thanks for everything in your life, God will help you to find contentment.

How Do You Find Time for Yourself?

These all sound like fine ideas, but some days I don't have time to take a shower until nap time. How in the world can I find time to work on these different dimensions of myself? It may be a very long time before you have uninterrupted time. Don't keep putting things off because you don't have several hours to do them. Instead, write down your goals or projects and figure out how you can do them in small bits of time. I have learned that even if I don't have a large chunk of time, I can still do my writing projects by using minutes.

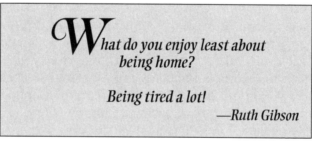

What do you enjoy least about being home?

Being tired a lot!

—Ruth Gibson

My husband wanted to upgrade our computer because we were both doing quite a bit of writing. But writing on the computer doesn't fit my time schedule. I rarely have time to sit uninterrupted in front of the computer. Instead, I write with a pencil on notebook paper attached to a wooden clipboard. It's always with me, and I can work at something a bit at a time. Over a period of time, those bits add up!

Do you hesitate to get involved with a project just for you because you sometimes feel like the maid in your house? Author Christine Davidson says, "Do the basics, keep the place sanitary, and save as much money as you can by doing things the old-fashioned way. But most of all, enjoy the job. When you're not enjoying it because of an overdose, find someone to look after your children for an hour or more and get out."[4]

Your husband will be the main person to help you find time for yourself. Think of creative ways to get some personal time. Denise Wickline says her husband and daughter go on "Daddy dates. He builds it up with her, and it's their big secret plan to do something wonderful together. They create great memories and it's a great relationship builder." It's also a great way for mom to get some time alone! Conversely, you should also make sure your husband has ample opportunity to take breaks from being a daddy in the evening.

If your husband is gone a lot, find a friend you can trade child care with or a reliable neighborhood baby-sitter. It may cost you a few dollars, but it can help you be a better wife and mother. Dannette Kaschalk puts it this way: "If you only give out, you run out of gas and can't give any more to your family without being resentful, hostile, and crabby." Mary Hotwagner, another mom at home, says, "I have learned that I am much less appealing to be around if I don't have time for me. It's not fair to me, the kids, or my husband."

What do other women do to sharpen the saw? In my surveys, exercise came up more than anything else. Debbi Heinze walks in the morning before anyone else in the family gets up. Then she steals time while the kids are watching TV or playing to read or cross stitch. Caron LaPlante says, "My main release is exercise. My children actually benefit from it because I am a more contented mother."

Marnie Murray, mom at home and devout Catholic, says she used to feel guilty about taking time for herself, "Until I decided that if I'm stressed and crabby, the whole house is stressed and crabby." She says going to mass daily really helps her cope, as does going to a YMCA where child care is provided while she exercises.

Cindy McCabe exercises, goes to the cheap movie theater
with a friend, and takes at least one week a year by herself. She
says, "One of the best pieces of advice I received from a
F.E.M.A.L.E. meeting was to treat parenthood as a job and take
at least two weeks off every year for rejuvenation. I take one
week with my husband and one week in free days or weekends
by myself. Your family respects you more and takes you less for
granted when you return."

If that doesn't sound realistic to you, how about a guilt-
free evening out for you while Daddy takes care of the kids?
Also, many parenting groups meet in the evening, which is
a double blessing—time away from the kids as well as some
conversation and encouragement for mom.

There are many ways you can find time for rejuvenation.
It could be as simple as taking turns with a neighbor so you
can each go for a walk alone while the other watches all the
children. Maybe it's getting up a little earlier to exercise and
have some devotional time. Look at the rhythm of your day
and see what works for you. Try something new to keep
your approach to the mothering season fresh.

We each have the same amount of time each day—
twenty-four hours. The difference between savoring the day
and getting everything done, and squandering your time is
a little planning, relaxing, and trusting.

Setting Goals

Sometimes my goal is to get to the end of the day. There
are lots of days like that. But did you ever think about
what your ideal day would be like? Taking time to daydream and pray about this may help you to set some long-
term goals.

You may not have articulated them, but you do have
goals. A goal is different than a to-do list. A to-do list fo-

cuses on the short-term requirements of running your family life. A goal is something quite different. For example, you probably have the goal of raising a happy, healthy family. You have the goal of supporting and encouraging your husband. You probably have other goals as well. Write them down. "Eighty percent of the people who commit their goals to writing accomplish them, while only twenty percent of those who have goals but don't write them down actually achieve them," says author Donna Otto.[5]

In your ideal day, what do you look like? Where do you live? What is your family like? How many children? What do you do all day? In your daydreaming, begin to work backwards to figure out what you need to do to reach your ideal day or goals. This can be an exciting journey of self-discovery. Perhaps you don't know what you would like to do next in your life. By allowing yourself to daydream and free associate about your likes, interests, and ambitions, you may come up with a new dream for your life.

Author Pamela Piljac suggests taking the following elements and setting a series of goals for each for three months, one year, five years, and ten years.[6] You can use the daydreaming you did above to develop these categories. This exercise will give you an excellent idea of what you need to do to reach your goals. Here are my current three month goals:

Three Month Goals

Marriage. Schedule a weekly time with spouse.
Lifestyle. Set a daily time limit on TV viewing.
Home. Sort and discard books and clothes.
Family. Plan one outing per week with everyone.
Physical. Walk three times a week.
Children. Spend ten minutes per day on phonics.

Intellect. Read magazine articles I've clipped.

Community. Plan the block party.

Professional. Send for information from associations.

Material. Purchase a used sofa.

Health. Get allergy shots regularly.

Social. Bring welcome basket to new neighbors.

Spiritual. Attend Wednesday prayer service.

Financial. Keep spending record; shop for computer program to organize records.

Friendship. Have lunch with two friends.

When you wrote your lists, did you find that you already have some of the elements of your ideal life? Give thanks to your God for arranging things so wonderfully! I am regularly overcome with gratitude when I look at my life and think of all the blessings he has sent to me.

Linda Dillow, who encourages us to be creative counterparts in our marriages, asks, "What is your goal in life? Do you even have one? Most of us don't think in terms of a lifetime; we're concerned about getting the laundry done on Monday and getting tonight's dinner on the table. Take a minute right now and write in one paragraph or less your life goal. I've thought a lot about this and have decided that, simply stated, my goal is to be a godly woman, to be all that God wants me to be as a woman, wife, and mother."[7] What a wonderful goal! Could you commit yourself to the same?

As you go through a goal-setting process, keep in mind that they aren't written in stone. Be flexible and willing to change. And always be tuned in to what God wants to do in your life. These are the goals and aspirations that will ring the truest and that God will help you accomplish.

Should I Volunteer My Time?

Volunteers are the backbone of many organizations. Without volunteers, there would be no Sunday school, no Awana, no Girl Scouts, and no PTA. Volunteering can provide the mother at home with needed outside stimulation and a chance to use other skills.

There are several factors to consider before making a commitment to become a volunteer. Consider whether you can do the work at home or if it will require a great deal of time away from the family. If it requires hours away from home, can you arrange child care and not detract from everything that needs to be done at home?

Another consideration is whether the work will give you an opportunity to polish or develop a skill that could be used at another time in your life. If a volunteer position will lead you in a new direction in your life when you are done with your season at home, it may be well worth your while.

There is a great deal of pressure for Christian women to volunteer their time. There are so many needs, even just in your sphere of friends at church. Don't forget the need to balance your desire to serve others with your primary responsibility to serve your family. If a volunteer project will take away from what you are trying to do at home, learn to say no.

Here are some places where you could volunteer:

- *Church.* Sunday school, nursery, women's groups, cooking meals for special needs, or providing hospitality for special events.
- *Community.* Teaching adult literacy, fundraising for charity, helping at a food bank or shelter, or serving on a city or village board or committee.
- *Hospitals.* Visiting the sick in hospitals or nursing homes.
- *Schools.* PTA organizations, being a room mom, helping with lunch, or supervising a field trip.

- *Prisons.* Corresponding with inmates to help lead them to the Lord.
- *Environment.* Working at a recycling center or working at a pet shelter.
- *The arts.* Leading an art or music group or planning an arts festival.

13

Enjoying the Family

Becoming a mother emphasized my own feelings of motherlessness. Where do you go to learn to be a mom? I picked the brains of the mothers I knew and devoured books on parenting, the psychology of motherhood, and mother/daughter relationships. I was fully prepared to overcompensate for the lackings in my own childhood to do a better job raising our children.

But I was so consumed with trying to give them everything I had not received as a child that I realized I was not allowing them to be sad, cranky, disillusioned, or disappointed. "Be happy!" I admonished them. I tried to control them and insist that they be well adjusted and constantly cheerful.

But I discovered I can allow them to feel their feelings and figure out what those feelings mean. I can be there for them to talk or cry when they need to. I can let them express the good and the bad about growing up, and help them figure it out. They are not motherless. My past is not their reality. Perhaps most importantly, I can learn to trust that God has a plan for their lives, just as he has for mine, and that my constant intervention is not always required. The Bible says, "I will put my trust in him. . . . Here am I, and the children God has given me" (Heb. 2:13). When I pray for them, I can give their lives to the Lord and ask him to touch their hearts and to guide me in the best way to raise them. When I totally gave them to the Lord, much of my confusion cleared. Their heavenly Father looks after them and has given me the job to watch over them here on earth. But how does a mom do that?

First I thought I had to primarily be a teacher. I spent lots of money on school curriculum-type books and tried to plan our days like a school day, even before my kids were old enough for home schooling. On a Monday we would play shapes games and make no-bake oatmeal cookies. However, on Monday our two little girls wanted to watch Barney and play with Play-Doh. I ended up feeling frustrated and unappreciated, and our kids felt pressured and confused.

Then I thought I just had to be a baby-sitter. My role was to provide the kids with some good play materials and just let them be. The problem with this approach was that I wanted more interaction with them, and they were clearly asking me for the same.

After a year of being at home, we finally hit upon a balance in the structure of our days, as well as in my mothering philosophy.

The Fun Stuff about Being Home

Each month, I make a list of activities we might want to do that month. It is usually based on seasons or holidays. I find that if I don't write them down, I don't come up with good ideas when I'm tired, or I might forget some really good activities. (I have to write virtually everything down, or it is lost in my mother's memory!) The list is loosely structured and usually includes at least a few field trip ideas.

Whenever we need something to do, we dip into our resources and come up with something special. In addition, there is great value in asking your kids, "What would you like to do?" When they direct the play or activity, it has special meaning to them. The trick again is finding balance. Too much activity and too much running around causes overscheduled and stressed-out kids. Jewel Wolfe, a mom at home, says, "I was finding that if I had too many mornings booked with activities that we were rushing off to that it was as stressful as if I were working."

Philosophically, my mothering has changed with the realization that children are learning all the time, not just when I am sitting down with them with a color wheel or alphabet flash cards. They are learning about how to manage stress when they see how I react to a crazy, busy day full of chores and errands. On an ideal day, they help me sort clothes, and we sing silly songs in the car. On a bad day, they hear a little too much yelling and are told too many times to "Hurry up!"

They are learning about compassion when they see how I react to their moods and needs, or when they see how I talk to a friend who calls on the phone and needs to talk when I am in a whirl of busyness. Do I take the time to affirm our daughters and raise their spirits, or do I tell them to go and play? Do I listen sincerely to my girlfriend's problems, or do I roll my eyes and try to get her off the phone? Our children's eyes are watching and studying all the time.

They are learning about honesty when they see what I do about the can of tuna the store checker forgot to scan in the bottom of my cart or when I receive too much change back from another store. They learn that it's worth making the effort to rectify the wrong, no matter how tiny, because that's how we do things in this family.

And they are learning about loving the Lord when we make sure we all get up in time for Sunday school or when we read them their take-home papers or their children's Bible at home. The biggest lessons our kids learn are the inadvertent ones. The biggest lesson I have learned about being a good mom is to pay attention to the everyday moments because our kids are watching all the time.

We are counseled in books and magazines to concentrate on our mothering. Am I doing a good job? Am I doing the right thing? But there is great value in shifting our gaze from ourselves to our children. Instead of analyzing ourselves and them, how about just enjoying them? The snapshots that are embedded in my memory are the unplanned, unpremeditated moments. I can see the sunshine on Clare's hair as she runs in the backyard, beaming a smile at me over her shoulder. I can see Caitlin dancing at an outdoor concert and telling me that she couldn't stop because she had "happy feet." I can see Clare creating out of the strangest things—like making pretend brides out of pencils and tissues. I can see Caitlin at the dinner table pointing to each of us in turn and saying, "I love you and you and you and me."

The really fun stuff about being home is the stuff that can't be engineered. I *love* going places, doing things, and having adventures with our kids. I think I'm giving them a well-rounded exposure to the world with a balance of planned and unplanned activities. My photo scrapbook may be filled with pictures of special trips, beautiful Christmas trees, and chubby fingers displaying their latest craft, but my memory book is crammed with mornings when we stayed in our pajamas until noon just because we were having too much fun.

Children take time. They need quantity time, not just quality time. A bubble bath, a shared bowl of soup, or a relaxing hair brushing can be the sweetest moments. Can we slow down enough to enjoy them? Can we block out our to-do list and shut off our worries and just savor the short season that we have with our small children? We can't bring it back. Our children won't wait to grow up while we work on one more project, or try one more case, or open one more account. They will grow up in spite of us. But what are we missing if we don't take the time to enjoy their childhoods? This chapter is dedicated to giving you ideas to enrich your time together.

Community Resources

The town I live in is one of the best places in America to raise children. There are so many activities and opportunities here that it takes careful thought and prayer to make sure we don't overschedule. When we were preparing to move here, I began my research into the community by browsing through a phone book and sending for literature from different organizations, and I obtained a wealth of information about the resources available in our area.

> *What do you enjoy most about being home?*
>
> *The unexpectedness of each day—every day unfolds differently.*
> —Patty Bruzek

Also before we physically moved, I visited the library and got a card. The town we lived in previously had a tiny one, but our county now has a system of absolutely wonderful libraries. They all use individual bar codes, and the back of my library card looks like a travel brochure because it has so many.

Each library has something to offer children and families and residency is not always required. Our town library has weekly story hours for children from age two to kindergarten, a short movie every Saturday, and a special storyteller or puppet show for the children several times a year. They also have summer reading programs and activities.

From a money-saving perspective, your library can save you a fortune on book purchases. Many libraries will put you on a waiting list to borrow the best-sellers. Other books are readily available. I keep a list in my calendar of titles I have come across that I want to read, and I check at the library first before I even consider purchasing a book. Keep in mind that your library also has an acquisition budget. If you want a particular title, ask your librarian to order it. They may appreciate the input, and you may get to read the books you really want to read. Your library can also provide you with magazines (saving you a fortune on subscriptions), how-to books, popular paperbacks, records, tapes, games, puzzles, movies, and even art. Ours has a virtual art gallery of framed prints and small sculptures that can be rented for eight weeks for two dollars.

Your park district can also be a source of some wonderful classes or instruction for your children. Gone are the days when park districts merely sponsored team sports. Now they offer classes in everything from ballet to pottery. Ours even has a preschool program and several other craft and activity classes for the little ones. They also do special events, like breakfast with Santa or the Easter Bunny. You also may want to investigate whether your area has an active forest preserve district, which would probably be listed in your phone book under the name of your county. Our forest preserve district has a number of nature centers and classes for all ages of children. An outing to one of these places can be a day-long nature adventure.

For local recreation and exercise, the YMCA may be your best value. Many offer a reasonable family rate as well as baby-sitting for smaller children. Ours has a family swim night and a family open gym. Your local YMCA could be a great resource for quality activities you can do with your children.

You may also want to write to local hospitals to see if they have classes or programs of interest to your family. In our old town, one of the local hospitals had a drop-in center for mothers that was open two mornings a week. Sometimes they had a speaker or program, and sometimes we just sat with coffee and needlework. They also had an extensive lending library and a parenting expert on hand who coordinated the program and answered questions. What a gem of a resource for a new parent!

Your town's Chamber of Commerce or downtown business group can let you know about special events, like parades or festivals. They typically also have information about the smaller, more hidden attractions in your area.

Play Space and Toys

Are toys taking over your house? Those little pieces really hurt when you step on them with bare feet! I have learned that toy management is a process. You have to train yourself to not overbuy, to move toys around, and to weed them out.

Susan Fenton, a mom at home, says it is important to "Weed things out often." Another mom, Nancy V., says: "Keep some toys put away in a closet and rotate them on occasion with other toys." Another toy trick comes from Rene Jurkowski, mom at home. She says, "I also save a few small toys that my daughter only sees when we go out to a restaurant that occupy her after she's done eating so we can finish eating." The novelty factor keeps her entertained and they can eat in peace.

You also have to train your children to pick up after themselves. Jodi Benware says, "I teach my kids how to help clean up their toys. They know if they get a lot of toys out, they'll have a lot to put away." Lori Solyom, a mom at home with three daughters, says she uses a series of plastic crates and colorful cardboard storage boxes in her family room. "Each container holds a different type of toy: puzzles, games, Barbie dolls, and art supplies. When things get out of control, we gather everything into one pile and do a massive sort." Lisa Munsterman, a mom at home, has these storage ideas:

- Use an under-bed container for Barbie dolls and their clothes.
- A fishing tackle box with compartments is great for storing toys with lots of small pieces.
- Use a mesh bag for tub toys, and hang it over the spigot to dry the toys after a bath.
- Collect syrup bottles, detergent scoops, and buckets for the beach or the pool—if any get lost, no big deal.

The Magic Closet

I hope our children will remember our house as a fun place to be. They have to learn responsibility and good behavior, but I want them to also know the meaning of joy in their lives. Sometimes I tell the girls, "I'm not having enough fun today. Let's do something about it." They are usually feeling the same way, so we use our resources.

I have a special extra closet in one of our rooms. If you don't have an extra closet, a box or even a paper bag will work. We call ours the magic closet. Inside are all our craft materials (defined as almost anything!), odds and ends, and little toys or treats I have picked up along the way, usually at the dollar store.

The girls love to do what they call "projects," which can be almost anything. So when they announce their desire to do projects, we open the magic closet and see what we can find. It might be an old seed catalog from which we cut and paste pictures of flowers. It might be a box of buttons to touch and sort. The end result might be a feather collage, or it might just be a mess on the table. When you go to the magic closet, you never know! We like this kind of open-ended project that the kids direct and complete the way they see fit.

Felt Boards

When our girls were younger, I saw some wonderful things in teacher stores that I wanted for my home, including felt boards. But they were so expensive, I decided to improvise. I love telling stories with felt boards or making up my own puzzles. I made my felt board by purchasing a huge piece of white felt and wrapping and taping it around a collapsed, sturdy cardboard box. We lean it up against something or use it lying flat on the table. And felt squares are incredibly cheap and versatile. You can sometimes pick them up for four or five for a dollar. They come in seasonal colors, too.

Some of the things we have made from felt for the felt board are an ABC puzzle, a shapes puzzle, felt ornaments for a felt Christmas tree that can be decorated and redecorated, a large snowman with a carrot nose and a black hat, and a variety of pumpkins with many expressions.

You can also use paper pictures or cut outs with felt boards by applying a small piece of Velcro to the back of the paper. The paper then adheres nicely to the felt, and you have lots of possibilities for displaying pictures or telling stories.

Blackboard

Get the biggest, nicest blackboard your house can accommodate. Our kids love drawing with chalk and then erasing. Provide them with different colors and an eraser, and they can spend hours drawing, writing, and erasing. You can also get a marker board for this type of activity. Either blackboards or marker boards can be purchased with an easel, and kids seem to enjoy standing up to write or create.

Seasons Tree

I love living in the Midwest because I can watch and commemorate the changing seasons. One fall, we went for a walk and found the most interesting branch we could find. It had lots of little branches on it and was just the right height. We took it home, put some old Play-Doh in the bottom of a small coffee can, and planted our seasons tree. The dough dried out in a few days and was able to hold the tree up. This tree not only provides a neat, homemade decoration for our house but also gives us an opportunity to discuss the seasons and holidays.

We use construction paper, yarn, markers, paint, or crayons to make seasonal decorations. At Christmas, we use cookie cutters to make ornaments. For Valentine's Day, we hang the tree with hearts. We especially enjoy the fall when we can make and decorate beautiful leaves. (Our favorite technique is to marble paint—put the paper in a box top, put a few globs of paint on it, and roll some marbles around for a very interesting effect.)

Window Stickers

We discovered Stik-ees a few years ago. They are plastic, removable stickers for windows, doors, or mirrors that come in a variety of patterns and collections. There are holiday Stik-ees, geometric ones for making your own creations, a doll set with clothing and furniture, and traditional ABCs and numbers. Our kids spend hours at the front window decorating and redecorating with Stik-ees. Other types of plastic pieces are available at your craft store, or you may order a Stik-ees catalog at the address below:

> Stik-ees
> 1165 Joshua Way
> P. O. Box 9630
> Vista, CA 92085-9630
> 1-800-441-0041

Quiet Bags

Quiet bags are packed by the children for car trips or going to places where they have to be quiet. I made simple drawstring bags for the girls out of some leftover material. Clare's is made from material for a doll dress. Caitlin's is made from her bedroom curtain material.

When we go on a trip, I pack a few lollipops, crayons, coloring books, paper, books, and any other items they request. When we go to a place where they have to be quiet (like orchestra practice), they pack their favorite dolls or whatever project they're involved in when it is time to leave the house. They love having their own bags!

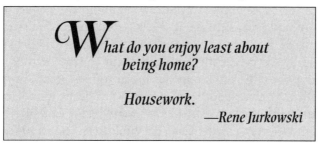

What do you enjoy least about being home?

Housework.

—Rene Jurkowski

Children's Bibles and Devotionals

Our best resource for devotional materials for our children is their Sunday school teacher. Do your children have take-home papers? Make it a point to read those papers during the week. Some have extra activities on them to do at home. This is a great way to keep your children interested in Sunday school and what is taught there.

Other than their papers, our favorite book is called *Little Visits 1–2–3* by Mary Manz Simon (St. Louis: Concordia Publishing House, 1990). Our children are young (three and four), but this book is perfect for their age level. The book includes about a dozen devotionals for each month. They are in the form of a simple poem or narrative and include suggestions for a simple prayer for each day. This is a delightful first devotional book for young children. The pictures are black and white line drawings, and I have allowed our children to color in this book with their markers. It is now truly personalized for them.

The best story Bible for children to read that I have found is *The Early Reader's Bible* by V. Gilbert Beers (Sisters, Oreg.: Questar Publishers, Inc., 1991). The Bible stories are told with simple language and include bright pictures. This is one of the books we use when we sit down to read a Bible story, and the children usually ask for more than one.

Another classic Bible storybook that we only recently discovered is *The Bible in Pictures for Little Eyes* by Kenneth Taylor (Chicago: Moody Press, 1984). Each Bible story has a paragraph of text and a picture explaining the event. Two or three questions follow to help you discuss what is happening in the story with your child. The exact biblical reference is also given, if your child wants to read further. We are enjoying this book a lot with our four-year-old.

We came across another good book in a home school reading curriculum. It is called *What Would Jesus Do?* by Mack Thomas (Sisters, Oreg.: Questar Publishers, Inc., 1991) and is a retelling of Charles M. Sheldon's classic book, *In His Steps.* This is a chapter book, and I expected that we would sit and read one chapter a night for twenty nights in a row. But we read the whole thing in one sitting, and the kids frequently ask to hear it again. This is a good transition book for moving from single storybooks to chapter books. In addition, the message is timeless—What would Jesus do in various situations? What would Jesus want *us* to do?

Finally, we bought our children Bibles last Christmas because we wanted them to have their own. We chose *The Children's Living Bible* (Wheaton, Ill.: Tyndale House Publishers, 1971) for two reasons. First, it includes several pages of illustrations that are similar to the ones our children have seen time and time again in their Sunday school curriculum, so we felt that they would feel familiar with this Bible. Second, it has a handle on it, so little hands can easily carry it around.

14

On Home Schooling

Perhaps one of the most difficult decisions we will make as parents is how and where to educate our children. There are many wonderful Christian schools in this country, but their cost may be prohibitive. You may have a local public school that is adequate, but you are concerned about the values your child will soak up in a public school atmosphere.

Home schooling is a marvelous alternative. It has been around since the beginning of time and is enjoying a resurgence in our day due to the challenges and difficulties of our culture. If you have never considered this alternative, you will be stunned, as I was, to uncover the support, resources, and enthusiasm of the home schooling community.

Why Home School?

Some of the most commonly stated reasons for home schooling include the following:

Flexibility. Families can set their own daily schedule and can take vacations or time away when they want. They are not restricted by the traditional school calendar. In addition, the children are able to learn at their own pace, when they are developmentally ready.

Values. Many home schoolers have strong religious beliefs or values that they wish to impart to their children in a home environment. One mom, Norma Kunda, refers to a "spiritual vacuum" in the public schools. She says, "We firmly believe God has given the primary responsibility for the education and upbringing of a child to his parents."

Peer threats. Education at home eliminates the fears parents have about violence and drugs in the schools.

More efficient use of time. Many home schoolers feel that six hours a day in a classroom is ridiculous for a young child. The same academic results can be obtained at home in a few hours per day.

Educating the family together. Jackie Wellwood, a home schooling mother of five, says, "We do not want to separate our children from each other during the educational process. Part of the process is that they are together learning how to relate to and care for each other."

Greater one-on-one attention. The child taught at home receives far more individual attention than the child taught in the traditional school setting.

Academic and personal results. Children who are home schooled perform well on standardized tests, and many are accepted to traditional colleges. Children learn to be internally motivated and responsible. Many home schooling parents see public education as a dismal failure in academic or social terms.

Diane Sergeant says she home schools so that each of her children may progress in each subject at their own speed and so she can teach Christian values and avoid humanistic philosophy. Another mom echoed Diane and added that she wanted her boys to have plenty of time to play and be creative. Cheryl Anderson appreciates that she can move her children more quickly on their own, eliminate "busy work," and focus on academics, not social programs and politically correct topics.

Marilyn Tabbut adds that home schooling is good stewardship, noting, "We believe that it is the parents' primary responsibility to educate their children. We believe that children, being a gift of God, are not ours to keep but have been given to us by God. When we hand over our children to any educational institution, public or private, it is critical that values and philosophy are consistent with what we believe." She also feels that home schooling will help "to raise responsible leaders for the next generation who will stand firm on their biblical convictions, who believe there is a right and wrong, and who will be able to rightly decide the truth." All of these women are members of a local home school support group, have home educated their children from three to ten years, and speak from experience.

Mary Pride is a mother and writer who is one of the most prolific, enthusiastic, and informed spokespeople for home schooling. She has written several resource books under the title of *The Big Book of Home Learning* that are a good starting point for shopping for home schooling materials. She is funny and easy to read, and you will learn much from any of her books. She notes that the advantages of learning at home are price, options, and freedom.[1] Boiled down to its essence, aren't these the greatest concerns most parents have about their children's education?

Making the Decision

One of the best resources that helped us make our initial decision about the education of our children is called *Schooling Choices: An Examination of Private, Public & Home Educa-*

tion.[2] It presents the views and rationales of three educators who each support one philosophy—Christian school, home schooling, or public school. Kenneth Gangel, chairman of the Department of Christian Education at Dallas Theological Seminary, writes about Christian schools. Gregg Harris, founding director of Christian Life Workshops and author of *The Christian Home School* (Brentwood, Tenn.: Wolgemuth & Hyatt, 1987), advocates on behalf of home schooling. David Smith, public school superintendent and educator for over twenty years in Illinois and Indiana, writes about public education.

> *W*hat do you enjoy most about being home?
>
> *I enjoyed nursing babies, playing with them, visiting friends, and entertaining.*
> —Ruth Gibson

For each option, the educators examine (among other things) whether there is a biblical basis for the method of education, the spiritual advantages, the educational advantages, how the child will benefit socially from the method, how the family will benefit, how society benefits, and what you need to know about financing for each choice. The book doesn't draw a conclusion for you and doesn't favor one option over another. Rather, each option is evaluated objectively by well-qualified educators who are thoroughly convinced of their positions.

Another excellent resource for decision-making is *Schooling Options: Choosing the Best for You and Your Child* by Elaine K. McEwan.[3] She reviews six steps to consider when you begin to look at your educational choices:

1. Determine what you believe the role of schooling should be in your child's life.
2. Consider your child and his or her special needs, interests, and talents.
3. Enumerate your own specific gifts and talents.
4. Understand the advantages and disadvantages of each schooling option.
5. Look at the specific options open to you and make a decision.
6. Monitor and evaluate your child's schooling process.

This very hands-on approach to decision making includes checklist exercises to help you determine the goals you hope are achieved by education. Two parent profile checklists will help you evaluate whether you are suited to home schooling or if the Christian or public school option is better for you. For example, if you are poorly organized and require lots of adult contact, home schooling might not be the best choice. On the other hand, if you love doing art projects at the dining room table and want to be intimately involved in every aspect of your child's life, then keep investigating home schooling. The basis of this approach is to know yourself and your child.

A classic work on home schooling by Ray E. Ballman is *The How and Why of Home Schooling*. According to Ballman, the answer to the question of whether home schooling is for you should be a resounding *yes* if you agree with these five, basic convictions:

1. I believe that God and patriotism should still hold a vital place in the classroom.
2. The development and growth of my child's delicate self-respect is very important to me.
3. I want to continue a special bond of closeness between me and my child.

4. As a parent, I have more of my child's best interest at heart than anyone else.
5. I am willing to embrace both my parental (in light of Scripture) and constitutional rights.[4]

Try It!

If your children are preschool age or younger, you have nothing to lose by experimenting with the home school lifestyle now. Purchase a book of preschooler activities or invest in a preschool curriculum and try it out with your children. This experiment will help you make a more informed decision. I have talked with women who, before they began home schooling, spoke wistfully about the family joy they would experience, only to learn later that the kids were sulking and hated it and mom was overinvested and felt unappreciated. Home schooling is not the only option. A trial period at home while your children are small is the best way to evaluate this option.

Other than experimenting, be sure to read, read, read, and send away for lots of literature, catalogs, and magazines. There are also home school support groups across the country. Even before making our decision, I joined my local group and got access to a lending library, a newsletter, and a curriculum fair. I also had the chance to meet and talk to many home schoolers—all for fifteen dollars per year. If you would like to find out more about the legality of home schooling or receive assistance in finding a support group, contact the Home School Legal Defense Association, P.O. Box 2091, Washington, D.C., 20013.

Remember, God is in charge of your child's life. He can turn it to good, regardless of where (or if) he goes to school. It is you and your family who are charged with teaching him values and Christian living. If you do this and pray for your child to seek God's guidance every step of the way, you will be doing the best for your child.

What do you enjoy most about being home?

Being there when my daughter does all the "firsts" and playing with her—seeing the world through a child's eyes.
—Rene Jurkowski

Sources of Home Schooling Information

Books

Home Schooling for Excellence, by David and Micki Colfax (Philo, Calif.: Mountain House Press, 1987). This is the delightful story of the Colfax family's four children and their home schooling odyssey. It presents not only their personal experience but also general advice and selected resources.

Family Matters: Why Home Schooling Makes Sense, by David Guterson (New York: Harcourt, Brace, Jovanovich, 1992). This book was written by a public school English teacher who home schools his children. It is a compelling, well written, convicting discussion of why home schooling makes sense.

Teach Your Own, by John Holt (New York: Delacorte Press, 1981). John Holt was one of the most prominent modern thinkers in the field of home education. This is a great introduction to the home school philosophy.

Home Spun Schools, by Raymond and Dorothy Moore (Waco: Word Books, 1982). The Moores are pioneers in the home school movement. This book provides some case histories of parents who pursued this rewarding alternative as well as some other valuable resource material.

Home Grown Kids, by Raymond & Dorothy Moore (Waco: Word Books, 1981). This is the Moore's practical handbook full of ideas and encouragement for teaching children at home.

The Big Book of Home Learning, four volume set by Mary Pride (Wheaton: Crossway Books, 1990). Mary Pride has written a series of books that are a great place to get started, browse, and educate yourself. The set includes: *Volume 1: Getting Started, Volume 2: Preschool and Elementary, Volume 3: Teen and Adult,* and *Volume 4: Afterschooling and Extras.* Each book reviews curriculum, other books, and correspondence schools.

The Home School Manual, by Theodore E. Wade (Auburn, Calif.: Gazelle Publications, 1991). This excellent introduction to home schooling is devoted to principles of home education and includes direct advice on specific areas of learning as well as turning theory into practice.

Organizations and Publications

Christian Life Workshops, P.O. Box 2250, Gresham, OR 97030. Phone (503) 667-3942. This organization is headed by Gregg Harris, one of the movement's primary spokespeople. They give seminars and sell workshops on audio cassette. Their brochure also features organizers and other books on home schooling.

Home School Legal Defense Association, P.O. Box 159, Paeonian Springs, VA 22139. Phone (540) 882-3838. This organization provides information on the legality of home schooling and legal challenges being faced across the nation. Members will receive legal representation if their home schooling is questioned in court.

Growing Without Schooling, 2269 Massachusetts Avenue, Cambridge, MA 02140. Phone (617) 864-3100. This bimonthly newsletter provides ideas and resources. Many home schoolers say it is quite useful.

The Teaching Home Magazine, P.O. Box 20219, Portland, OR 97294-0219. Phone (503) 253-9633. This Christian home schooling magazine is a must for home schoolers.

This list is but a small sample of the materials available for home schoolers and is not intended to be exhaustive. Once you start digging around, you will be astounded at the materials and support available.

15

In Praise of Sequencing

And what do *you* do?"

The question inevitably arises at social functions. After eight years of practicing law and years of infertility, we were an instant family. I went from a total career orientation to being a full-time mother. I used to say, "I'm a lawyer, but now I'm at home with my children." After being home a little longer, I began to say, "I'm at home with my children, but I'm also a lawyer." I now have the courage of my convictions to say, "I'm a mother at home with my children." This conviction came only after I celebrated the one year anniversary of being home with our two small children.

There were hard choices to make. With the children only seventeen months apart, a new job for my husband, and moving across the state, I felt we were under enough stress. We bought the cheapest house we could find and kept the old cars running, and I became a full-time mother.

They call us the New Traditionalists. They call what we are doing sequencing. It means that we choose to "have it all, but not all at once."[1] Author Debbie Barr says this about sequencing: "It allows us to say 'I love you' to our children in the most convincing way possible: by being there during the season of their lives when they need the most nurture and physical care. . . . When we sequence, we can participate fully in each season of life, enjoying it and savoring its moments without regret or guilt. Sequencing gives us time to be the kind of mothers we want to be, and it gives us the opportunity to be—and to become—all that God has in mind for us."[2]

The leading proponent of this balanced lifestyle is Arlene Rossen Cardozo, author of the book *Sequencing*. She says:

> Sequencing is the solution more and more women choose of having it all—career and family—by not trying to do it all at once, at all times in their lives. Women who elect to sequence first complete their educations and gain career experience, then leave full-time work during the years they bear and mother their young children, and then—as their children grow—innovate new ways to incorporate professional activities into their lives, so that mothering and profession don't conflict. . . . they are the first generation of women to be full-time mothers completely through choice.[3]

If our mothering is completely through choice, we must be prepared to choose it joyfully, mindful of the time and energy commitment required and single-minded in our concern for the welfare of our children.

Who sequences? It's not just women like myself. Some prominent examples of sequencers are none other than Supreme Court Justice Sandra Day O'Connor and former United Nations Ambassador Jeane Kirkpatrick.

Will you lag behind your contemporaries when you return to work? Perhaps. It may take you some time to achieve an income comparable to non-sequencers, but you will have accomplished much in your home. Many of us believe the tradeoffs are well worth it.

Authors Sanders and Bullen note, "It also is true that the longer you work, the more chance you will have to recoup from taking time off. With the mandatory retirement age being pushed back farther and farther, chances are good that you could devote twenty years to your children and still have twenty productive years in the paid workforce."[4] I am confident that the eight years I devoted to my career will be to my advantage when I return to practicing law. If an employer wants to hold my "parenting sabbatical" against me, then maybe their values are not adequately compatible to mine and theirs would not be the best work environment for me anyway.

Why sequence? Hopefully you have reached your own answers to that question by reading this book. Twenty benefits of being an at-home mom are eloquently summarized by authors Sanders and Bullen. Among the most compelling are not missing your child's childhood, having a deeper relationship with your child, and the feeling that raising your child is a job that really matters.

What do you enjoy most about being home?

The freedom to have a flexible schedule and to be able to be with my children as they grow and learn.
—Norma Kunda

Full-time, day-to-day life with children is very different from the work world. The transition from being in control in court or running an efficient law office to being home with free-spirited children was difficult. But by being home, I not only get to see the milestones of their development, I also get to feed our children their meals, read them multiple stories on demand, kiss their hurts, affirm their self-esteem, and help to lead them to the Lord on a daily basis.

Contrary to what some friends and colleagues prophesied, I have not gone crazy or become brain dead from "wasting all my education." Our children are giving me a whole different kind of education. I am learning to pay attention to the beautiful, small details of life. I am learning patience. I am learning to relax and enjoy the too short passage of childhood through the eyes of two small people who have some wonderful insights.

When asked how she felt about wasting her education, author Christine Davidson prided herself on this: "I became better at creative problem solving after two years at home than I was after six years of higher education. As a mother at home, I had to resist the temptation to solve a problem with money and instead had to think up as many solutions as I could. I really had to think."[5] Those of us who are maturing in motherhood can echo those sentiments. The things children teach us about creativity, human nature, the simple joy of living, and patience cannot be learned in any other arena. As for practicing law, there will always be acrimony and avarice. People will always have legal problems. It will all still be there when I am done raising our babies.

In my past profession, my days were full of seemingly weighty issues and hard decisions. Now, my days are full of small joys and wonders. I know in my heart that I have been given a wonderful gift and that mothering of our children is the highest and best use of my time and talents right now. I have learned that my current profession of motherhood takes work, dedication, and sacrifice, just as my former profession did. And every day I thank God that I realized early in our children's lives that the job he gave me to do was worth doing well and was worth my full commitment of energy and time.

Mothering at home is not for everyone, and I fully support those who strive to combine career with parenting. I am acquainted with both sides of this difficult decision. But, if you are the mother (or father) of a new or not-so-new little person who is tugging at your heartstrings to spend more time with them, *go for it*. As Dr. Brenda Hunter puts it, "This is time to dream a new dream."[6] If your dream is to build a home that is a haven of peace, rest, love, and acceptance for your children and husband, take a deep breath, ask God to guide you, and *do it!*

The popular media portrayal of sequencing, when it is mentioned at all, assumes that a mother will flee from home as soon as her children are sufficiently mature. But author Debbie Barr reminds us:

> A Christian view of sequencing must allow that motherhood, in and of itself, can be chosen as a career. Those women whose talents and interests are best suited to mothering, and whose best career choice therefore is mothering, deserve equal respect and acceptance. Their sequence, however, will look a little different.
>
> A Christian view of sequencing must also allow for something radical—the guidance of the Holy Spirit. When to stay at home, when to go to work, how to balance money and priorities with family needs—God alone can supply the kind of wisdom and direction parents need to make these decisions. The best implementation of sequencing will occur when mothers and fathers are on their knees, seeking God's plan for their family.[7]

If you are struggling with this decision, ask God for wisdom, and he will direct your path to the highest and best use of your gifts. If you have already made the decision, rejoice in the children God has given you to raise and cherish every moment with them.

Praying for Our Children

Our children need our time to raise them, our hands to help them, our hearts to love them, and our prayers to point them toward the Lord. Pray for your children. Pray that they will become godly men and women who will put their love for God first in their lives. Pray that they will come, at an early age, to a deep, personal relationship with Jesus which will sustain them through the trials of their growing years and endure through their lives. Pray that they will learn to trust in the Lord to guide their lives to paths and decisions that are pleasing to him.

*W*hat do you enjoy most about being home?

Being able to give them the security I didn't have as a child.
                                        —Dannette Kaschalk

Pray for your children every day. They belong to the Lord. He will show them, with your example, the way to a godly life. For a mother, no endeavor is more satisfying.

Notes

Chapter 1: Why I Went from Full-Time Lawyer to Full-Time Mom

1. Debbie Barr, *A Season at Home* (Grand Rapids: Zondervan Publishing House, 1993), 25.

2. Brenda Hunter, Ph.D., *Home by Choice* (Portland: Multnomah Press, 1991), 184.

Chapter 2: Why Stay Home?

1. John Bowlby, *Attachment and Loss* (New York: Basic Books, 1982), 177.

2. Hunter, *Home by Choice*, 29.

3. Ibid., 41.

4. Marilee Horton, *Free to Stay at Home* (Waco: Word Books, 1982), 52.

5. Robert Karen, "Becoming Attached," *Atlantic Monthly* (February 1990): 38.

6. Daniel Wattenberg, "The Parent Trap," *Insight Magazine* (March 2, 1992): 8.

7. Ibid., 9.

8. Barr, *A Season at Home*, 24.

9. Ibid., 37–38.

10. Donna Otto, *The Stay-at-Home Mom* (Eugene, Oreg.: Harvest House Publishers, 1991), 31–32.

11. Hunter, *Home by Choice*, 61.

12. Elizabeth Wurtzel, "Will I Ever Be Happy?" *Mademoiselle* (January 1994): 78.

13. Mary Ann Cahill, *The Heart Has Its Own Reasons* (Franklin Park, Ill.: La Leche League International, 1983), 31.

14. Christine Davidson, *Staying Home Instead* (Lexington, Mass.: Lexington Books, 1986), 39.

15. Ibid., 40.

16. Darcie Sanders and Martha Bullen, *Staying Home: From Full-Time Professional to Full-Time Parent* (Boston: Little, Brown & Co., 1992), 20.

17. Mary Pride, *The Way Home* (Wheaton: Crossway Books, 1985), 108–109, 111.

18. D. Ross Campbell, *How to Really Love Your Child* (Wheaton: Victor Books, 1986), 130.

19. Hunter, *Home by Choice*, 197.

20. Arlene Rossen Cardozo, *Sequencing* (New York: Collier Books, 1986), 163.

21. Hunter, *Home by Choice*, 107.

22. Wattenberg, "The Parent Trap," 11.

23. Otto, *The Stay-at-Home Mom*, 36–37.

24. Horton, *Free to Stay at Home*, 170.

25. Otto, *The Stay-at-Home Mom*, 29–30.

26. Pamela Piljac, *You Can Go Home Again* (Portage, Ind.: Bryce-Waterton Publications, 1985), 239–40.

27. Hunter, *Home by Choice*, 65.

28. Piljac, *You Can Go Home Again*, 240.

29. Davidson, *Staying Home Instead*, 12.

30. Sanders and Bullen, *Staying Home*, 21.

31. Hunter, *Home by Choice*, 192.

32. Harold Kushner, "The Biggest Mistake I Ever Made," *Reader's Digest* (July 1991): 69.

33. Otto, *The Stay-at-Home Mom*, 79.

34. Sanders and Bullen, *Staying Home*, 90.

35. Hunter, *Home by Choice*, 131.

36. David Elkind, *The Hurried Child: Growing Up Too Fast Too Soon* (Reading, Mass.: Addison-Wesley Publishing Co., 1981), 199.

37. Charles E. Hummel, *The Tyranny of the Urgent* (Downers Grove, Ill.: InterVarsity Press, 1967), 15.

38. Richard Swensen, M.D., *Margin* (Colorado Springs: NavPress, 1992), 160.

39. Hunter, *Home by Choice*, 47.

40. Ibid., 157.

41. Ibid., 166.

42. Linda Dillow, *Creative Counterpart* (Nashville: Thomas Nelson, Inc., 1977), 42.

Chapter 3: Can You Afford to Stay Home?

1. Otto, *The Stay-at-Home Mom*, 76.

2. Hunter, *Home By Choice*, 78.

3. Cardozo, *Sequencing*, 93–94.

4. Ibid., 2.

5. Cahill, *The Heart Has Its Own Reasons*, 10.

6. Sue Shellenbarger, "Job Costs Eat Up Second Paychecks," *The Wall Street Journal* (April 22, 1992): B1.

7. Sanders and Bullen, *Staying Home*, 26.

8. Swensen, *Margin*, 13.

9. Davidson, *Staying Home Instead*, 7.

10. Cahill, *The Heart Has Its Own Reasons*, 22.

11. Davidson, *Staying Home Instead*, 51.

12. Cahill, *The Heart Has Its Own Reasons*, 15.

13. Anita Jones-Lee, "Can You Afford to Quit?" *Parents Magazine*, (September 1992): 121.

14. Cahill, *The Heart Has Its Own Reasons*, 62.

15. Horton, *Free to Stay at Home*, 157.

Chapter 4: Making the Psychological Transformation

1. Cardozo, *Sequencing*, 120.
2. Cahill, *The Heart Has Its Own Reasons*, 2.
3. Cardozo, *Sequencing,* 117.
4. Otto, *The Stay-at-Home Mom*, 74.
5. Ibid., 69, 71.
6. Cardozo, *Sequencing*, 124.
7. Sanders and Bullen, *Staying Home*, 44.
8. Ibid., 34.
9. Cardozo, *Sequencing,* 87.
10. Ibid., 88, 117.
11. Ibid., 129.
12. Horton, *Free to Stay at Home*, 159
13. Cardozo, *Sequencing*, 107.
14. Horton, *Free to Stay at Home,* 64.

Chapter 5: What Happened to My Self-Esteem?

1. Dr. Evelyn Silten Bassoff, *Mothering Ourselves* (New York: A Dutton Book, 1991), 17.
2. Idene Goldman, 1993 Presentation to Wheaton-Earrenville Preschool PTA, Wheaton, Ill.
3. Linda Tschirhart Sanford and Mary Ellen Donovan, *Women and Self-Esteem* (Garden City, N.Y.: Anchor Press/Doubleday, 1984), 127–38.
4. Joyce Block, Ph.D., *Motherhood as Metamorphosis: Change and Continuity in the Life of a New Mother* (New York: A Dutton Book, 1990), 141.
5. Hunter, *Home by Choice*, 140.
6. Barr, *A Season at Home,* 24.

Chapter 6: You'll Always Be a Mother, but Your Kids Only Have One Childhood

1. Hunter, *Home by Choice*, 102.
2. Ibid., 103.
3. Dr. Anthony Moriarty, *Confronting Youth Gangs* (Matteson, Ill.: Psychological Resources, 1994), 12.

Chapter 7: The Mommy Wars

1. Davidson, *Staying Home Instead,* 143.
2. Piljac, *You Can Go Home Again*, 38.
3. Hunter, *Home by Choice*, 95.
4. Sanders and Bullen, *Staying Home,* 130.
5. Ibid., 130–31.
6. Linda Burton, Janet Dittmet, and Cheri Loveless, *What's a Smart Woman Like You Doing at Home?* (Vienna, Va.: Mothers at Home, 1992), 139–40.
7. Ibid., 151–59.

8. Alecia Swasy, "Stay-at-Home Moms Are Fashionable Again in Many Communities," *The Wall Street Journal* (July 23, 1993): 1.

9. Linda Rush, National Board of Directors of F.E.M.A.L.E., Private Letter of July 26, 1993.

10. Marilyn Gardner, "Working Mothers Who Stay Home," *The Christian Science Monitor* (August 18, 1992): 14.

11. Elena Neuman, "More Moms Are Homeward Bound," *Insight Magazine* (January 10, 1994): 16.

Chapter 8: Getting Support from Your Husband

1. Steven R. Covey, *Principle-Centered Leadership* (New York: Simon & Schuster, 1992), 142.

2. Ibid., 142.

3. *Personal Leadership Application Workbook* (Provo, Utah: Covey Leadership Center), 10.

4. Piljac, *You Can Go Home Again*, 136.

5. Campbell, *How to Really Love Your Child*, 19.

6. Otto, *The Stay-at-Home Mom*, 105.

7. John Bradshaw, *Bradshaw On: The Family* (Deerfield Beach, Fla.: Health Communications, Inc., 1988), 47.

8. Angela Elwell Hunt, "Friendship Is the Key," *Standard*, Kansas City, Mo. (February 20, 1994): 4.

Chapter 9: Finding Other Support

1. Valerie Bell, "Elisa Morgan: Mom's the Word," *Today's Christian Woman* (September/October 1993): 52.

2. Suzanne Hurt, "Nontraditional Caregivers Comfort Mothers to Be," *Wheaton Journal* (March 4, 1994): 22.

3. Elizabeth Berg, *Family Traditions* (Pleasantville, N.Y.: The Reader's Digest Association, Inc., 1992), 101.

4. Gloria Gaither and Shirley Dobson, *Let's Make a Memory* (Dallas: Word Publishing, 1983), 170.

5. Horton, *Free to Stay at Home*, 162–63.

6. Karen Moderow, "Moms at Home," *Moody Monthly* (February 1994): 13.

Chapter 10: Getting It All Done

1. Deniece Schofield, *Escape From the Kitchen* (Cincinnati: Writer's Digest Books, 1986).

2. Deniece Schofield, *Confessions of a Happily Organized Family* (Cincinnati: Writer's Digest Books, 1984), 72.

3. Mimi Wilson and Mary Beth Lagerborg, *Once a Month Cooking* (Colorado Springs: Focus on the Family Publishing, 1992), 2.

4. Jill Bond, *Dinner's in the Freezer!* (Lake Hamilton, Fla.: Reed Bond Books, 1993).

5. Olivia Wu, "Cooks' Co-op," *The Daily Herald* (February 3, 1994): 6.

6. Amy Dacyczyn, *The Tightwad Gazette* (New York: Random House, 1992), 57.

7. Cahill, *The Heart Has Its Own Reasons,* 127.

8. Deniece Schofield, *Confessions of an Organized Housewife* (Cincinnati: Writer's Digest Books, 1982), 48–49.

9. Davidson, *Staying Home Instead,* 62–63.

10. Ibid., 77.

Chapter 11: Finances

1. Swensen, *Margin,* 197.

2. Barr, *A Season at Home,* 192.

3. Horton, *Free to Stay at Home,* 149.

4. Cahill, *The Heart Has Its Own Reasons,* 247.

Chapter 12: Taking Care of Ourselves

1. Emilie Barnes, *Things Happen When Women Care* (Eugene, Oreg.: Harvest House Publishers, 1990), 22.

2. Otto, *The Stay-at-Home Mom,* 79.

3. Ibid., 39.

4. Davidson, *Staying Home Instead,* 80.

5. Otto, *The Stay-at-Home Mom,* 89.

6. Piljac, *You Can Go Home Again,* 187.

7. Dillow, *Creative Counterpart,* 43.

Chapter 14: On Home Schooling

1. Mary Pride, *The Big Book of Home Learning, Vol. 1* (Wheaton: Crossway Books, 1990), 17.

2. H. Wayne House, *Schooling Choices: An Examination of Private, Public & Home Education* (Portland: Multnomah, 1988).

3. Elaine K. McEwan, *Schooling Options: Choosing the Best for You and Your Child* (Wheaton: Harold Shaw Publishers, 1991).

4. Ray E. Ballman, *The How and Why of Home Schooling (Westchester, Ill.: Crossway Books, 1987),* 14.

Chapter 15: In Praise of Sequencing

1. Cardozo, *Sequencing,* 2.

2. Barr, *A Season at Home,* 26–27.

3. Cardozo, *Sequencing,* 17.

4. Sanders and Bullen, *Staying Home,* 186.

5. Davidson, *Staying Home Instead,* 72.

6. Hunter, *Home by Choice,* 186.

7. Barr, *A Season at Home,* 28.

About the Author

Christine Field is a former attorney, now a stay-at-home mom raising three daughters. She is a columnist for the F. E.M.A.L.E. Forum newsletter and lives in Wheaton, Illinois, with her husband and daughters.